ACKNOWLEDGMENTS

If we are honest with ourselves, we know that we all stand on the shoulders of those who have gone before us, as well as on the shoulders of those who continue to influence us. The most important influence in human life is the grace of God that daily touches life. I think God brings people into our lives and at the intersection of those relationships God's grace continuously grows and influences us. I give thanks to God for the people whose journeys have crossed mine.

Specifically I would like to thank Phill Martin and David Cassady, without whose help this book would still reside in the dark recesses of my computer hard drive. I appreciate the help of the staff and editors at Smyth & Helwys Publishing, and in particular Keith Gammons and Leslie Andres. I also thank my family, Diane, James, and Christine, for their support and love during this process and in our entire journey together. For all of the people who continue to influence me on my continuing journey I give thanks to God.

TELLING THE STORY

THE GOSPEL
IN A TECHNOLOGICAL AGE

J. STANLEY HARGRAVES

Smyth & Helwys Publishing, Inc.
6316 Peake Road
Macon, Georgia 31210-3960
1-800-747-3016
©2010 by Smyth & Helwys Publishing
All rights reserved.

Library of Congress Cataloging-in-Publication Data

Hargraves, J. Stanley.

Telling the story : the Gospel in a technological age / J. Stanley Hargraves.
p. cm. Includes bibliographical references and index.
ISBN 978-1-57312-550-5
1. Internet—Religious aspects—Christianity.
2. Internet in evangelistic work.
3. Internet in church work.
I. Title. BV3793.H349 2009 269'.202854678—dc22 2009047928

CONTENTS

INTRODUCTION

The church has a tale to tell. It is an ancient story that has come down through the ages to the present. Many different cultures and denominations tell different versions of the story, but the underlying theme is the same: that God has broken into human history to share with humanity an invitation to relationship. The writer of the Gospel of John says it this way: "For God so loved the world that he gave his only Son, so that everyone who believes in him may not perish but may have eternal life. Indeed, God did not send the Son into the world to condemn the world, but in order that the world might be saved through him."[1]

The story is not about condemnation, but about redemption. It is a story of hope that God has supplied a way for humanity to experience a relationship with God. While the church is the bearer of the story, the church did not create the story. The church shares the story as the teller, not the instigator. The telling of the story, or evangelism, is not redemptive or salvific in and of itself; instead, evangelism invites people into the story of God's love and grace in the world. In his book *Biblical Perspectives on Evangelism: Living in a Three-Storied Universe*, Walter Brueggemann argues that the Bible revolves around the stories of the promise to the Hebrew ancestors, the liberation from slavery in Egypt, and the gift of land to displaced peasants.

It is my argument that evangelism means inviting people into these stories as the definitional story of our life, and thereby authorizing people to give up, abandon, and renounce other stories that have shaped their lives in false or distorting ways. . . . Evangelism, I propose, is the invitation to re-imagine our lives in these narrative modes. The hearing of these narratives of reality makes us more inescapably aware that an attempt to live without the Holy Character of these narratives is indeed a life of "non-sense." . . . My understanding of evangelism as entry into the three stories invites us to re-experience and relive our lives according to the promise to the ancestors, the liberation of slaves, and the gift of land to displaced peasants.[2]

These three stories invite humanity to become part of the story in the contemporary world. The question for the church is how to tell the story in a way that invites people to re-image their lives in relationship to God. The church must invite people to become a chapter of the story rather than simply mimicking it or ignoring it as irrelevant. The church knows the story, or at least is invited to be a part of it, so how does it communicate that story to a world vastly different from the world of the first century? That is the task of the church today.

The church has existed for centuries by adapting to changing times the means of communicating the gospel. Often people like to think back on the "good old days," when life seemed better and simpler, the times when people think the church flourished more than it does today. Sometimes we all long for those times. The "good old days" are days within our own lifetimes and based on our personal experiences. We tend to forget that the church existed before those times and already underwent many eras of change. The point is that our earliest experiences of the church inform our faith and become meaningful to us. As new generations come into the church, not everything that is meaningful to previous generations will carry the same meaning for these newcomers. We must find a way to escape our nostalgia and greet the world with a fresh rendition of the gospel.

In the past, the church told the gospel story in meaningful and powerful ways for the people who heard it. From the advent of the printing press, which resulted in a simple means for reproducing Scripture, to musical instruments, to modern church buildings with LCD projectors and computers, the church has found ways of using what is available in the world to share Jesus Christ. Communication and technology are a means toward the end of telling the world about the grace of God manifest in Christ. Adapting that message to the available technology and language helps the church reach out in meaningful ways to people around the world.

How the church shares the story is important. People experience the gospel in many different forms, from the words used in telling the story to their experiences when they enter the sanctuary for the first time. Is the church able to translate the gospel into modernity such that people who have never heard it can experience something of the gracious invitation of God? When people look at the lives and actions of church members, are they able to see the living Christ? What the church does and says matters if the church is to reach out to people in relevant ways.

When people first come to church, the hospitality they experience determines how they hear the gospel story and helps them decide whether they will return. Body language, the words of welcome, and how guests are treated reveal how welcomed they are in the church community. Hospitality is more than a welcome bag or a time of greeting in the worship service. Hospitality begins at the church doors and goes home with guests so that they feel driven to return. Does the community of faith only welcome those inside the church, or is the church able to reach beyond the familiar to people who seek to understand and experience Christian community?

Is the church able to move beyond membership to discipleship so that people are welcomed and the life-changing story of the gospel is shared with everyone God sends into the church? The invitation to the gospel story is about more than joining a community of faith. The gospel story is a change in lifestyle that occurs over time and draws people closer to God. The church is not about making members; the church is about making *disciples*. If the church is unwilling to tell the story, experience tells us that God will find a way!

This book explores some of the biblical and theological themes related to the use of technology and resources for communicating the gospel in the modern world. The Bible is full of examples of God using the people and resources available at the present moment for the purposes of God. Human history also offers examples of people being used by God. As we explore ways the story has been told, we will discover that God uses many tools to introduce people to a meaningful and life-changing experience with God. Ultimately, God's story will be told and lives will be touched from our meager attempts at telling the story. However, we also must maintain the perspective that the church does not bring salvation to the world by telling the story; only God's sacrifice makes it possible. All the church can do is to find ways of sharing the story, knowing that only God has the power to touch human hearts. Even with all the technology and communication possibilities of the modern world, in the end people's experience of God and the faith community is relational. The church must explore ways of coming together as a community of faith that invites people into the story of God's grace.

NOTES

1. John 3:16-17. Scripture quotations, unless otherwise indicated, are from the NRSV.

2. Walter Brueggemann, *Biblical Perspectives on Evangelism: Living in a Three-Storied Universe* (Nashville: Abingdon Press, 1993) 10.

Chapter 1

THE CALL TO SPEAK

Now the eleven disciples went to Galilee, to the mountain to which Jesus had directed them. When they saw him, they worshiped him; but some doubted. And Jesus came and said to them, "All authority in heaven and on earth has been given to me. Go therefore and make disciples of all nations, baptizing them in the name of the Father and of the Son and of the Holy Spirit, and teaching them to obey everything that I have commanded you. And remember, I am with you always, to the end of the age." (Matt 28:16-20)

The church is called to tell the story. It is not an option; rather, it is part of the identity of being the church. It does not matter whether we fully understand the intricacies of the story. No matter what, we are called to tell the story. When Jesus delivered the Great Commission in Matthew, surely the disciples were on a religious high. Friday and Saturday were certainly difficult days as Jesus was crucified and buried, but Sunday had arrived. The resurrected Jesus appeared to them, and even at this high moment as they worshiped, some expressed doubt. What did they, who saw the risen Jesus face to face, doubt? The text does not deal with specifics, and Jesus does not seem concerned about it. Jesus does not chastise them or ask them to change their attitude. Jesus does not exclude them from the community of faith for their weakness. He commissions the believers and doubters together!

The story is not dependent on humanity's ability or faith. God can use even doubters to share the story with the world. It is God's story, and it will be told. Over and over, the church is instructed to go and share the good news. It is not merely about preparing for people to come and hear the story; it is also about going to people with the story. It is easy for the church to get caught up in different things, like building facilities, sponsoring programs, and raising funds, but often these things by themselves don't necessarily make disciples. The busyness of the church can often distract the church from sharing the gospel story and inviting people into a living relationship with Christ.

The church is given the radical challenge not of sitting around waiting for people to knock on the doors, but of going out into the world to proclaim God's love. It is important to explore why the church shares the story with the world, and biblical perspectives of the elements of sharing will help us expand our approach to the mission.

CALLED TO GO

The church is called to go out into the world. The church must go beyond the walls and even beyond the parking lot to proclaim the good news fully. While it is true that church members need to hear the good news, the church must also speak to those who may not know the location of the building. The good news must travel to the hurting and dispossessed in order to be effective.

For hundreds of years, the people of Israel languished in slavery in the land of Egypt. They lifted prayers and cried tears to God, begging for deliverance from bondage. In God's time, a deliverer was sent, but he was not the one we might expect. God came to Moses, who was born a Hebrew in Egypt but grew up in the palace of Pharaoh. His Hebrew heritage boiled over one day when Moses killed an Egyptian guard who beat a Hebrew slave. The next day, he intervened with two arguing Hebrews. In response, one of them replied, "Who made you a ruler and judge over us? Do you mean to kill me as you killed the Egyptian?" (Exod 2:14). Pharaoh discovered the murder and Moses escaped Egypt to live with relatives in Midian. He married the daughter of the priest of Midian and became a shepherd. While he tended sheep one day, God appeared in a burning bush and Moses began to negotiate.

> Then the LORD said, "I have observed the misery of my people who are in Egypt; I have heard their cry on account of their taskmasters. Indeed, I know their sufferings, and I have come down to deliver them from the Egyptians . . . . The cry of the Israelites has now come to me; I have also seen how the Egyptians oppress them. So come, I will send you to Pharaoh to bring my people, the Israelites, out of Egypt." But Moses said to God, "Who am I that I should go to Pharaoh, and bring the Israelites out of Egypt?" He said, "I will be with you; and this shall be the sign for you that it is I who sent you: when you have brought the people out of Egypt, you shall worship God on this mountain." But Moses said to God, "If I come to the Israelites and say to them, 'The God of your

ancestors has sent me to you,' and they ask me, 'What is his name?' what shall I say to them?" God said to Moses, "I AM WHO I AM." He said further, "Thus you shall say to the Israelites, 'I AM has sent me to you.'" God also said to Moses, "Thus you shall say to the Israelites, 'The LORD, the God of your ancestors, the God of Abraham, the God of Isaac, and the God of Jacob, has sent me to you': This is my name forever, and this my title for all generations. Go and assemble the elders of Israel, and say to them, 'The LORD, the God of your ancestors, the God of Abraham, of Isaac, and of Jacob, has appeared to me, saying: I have given heed to you and to what has been done to you in Egypt.'" (Exod 3:1-17)

Moses might not be our first choice as a deliverer of Hebrew slaves. He grew up in the palace rather than the slave quarters; he was wanted for murder by the Egyptians and perhaps not completely trusted by the Hebrew people, and yet God chose him above all others for the difficult task of bringing the people of Israel out of bondage. Moses had to face his past, including the killing of the guard, and he had to gain the respect of the Hebrew people. It was an awesome task, but God, not Moses, was the primary actor. God empowered Moses for the task. Whatever excuse Moses offered, God met it with a solution.

Despite Moses' hesitation, he had to go outside the confines of his exile to respond to the call of God to communicate good news and liberation. God's call to us is never easy. It calls us to go outside our comfort zones, meets our excuses with new solutions, and invites us to take risks for the sake of the realm of God. The mission of Moses and the mission of the church are about God reaching out to God's people. God's power, not human power, will proclaim the message. Moses could not continue to live in Midian and have any hope of freeing the people of Israel who lived in Egypt. He had to go back to Egypt, where the people ached in slavery. The message God gave Moses offered joy to some and caused difficulty for others, but he communicated the message to both Hebrew and Egyptian, giving both the opportunity to respond. The response was not always what Moses desired, but Moses could not make anyone respond as he wished. He moved one step at a time and waited for God's next move.

As Moses could not proclaim release from the mountains in Midian to the slaves in Egypt, so the church cannot communicate to the world from inside the church walls. It is certainly safer to do so, but the message and mission are not accomplished. To communicate effectively, one must reach out to where people are to share with them what God has done. The message of the church is joy to some and difficult for others, and the response is not always what the church or God would desire. Yet that is not an excuse to stop sharing the story. In the commissioning of the disciples in Matthew, Jesus does not tell the disciples to go only when and where they will be successful, but to go into the world. The mission of the church is about being faithful to the call of God in the lives of individual people as well as in the corporate body of the church. Such faithfulness may at times seem defeating, when in actuality it is divinely victorious. Certainly, the actions of Jesus in his life and on the cross remind us of a faithful life that appears to end tragically but is turned around by God. God is on the move in the world, and the church is called to proclaim the story while God continues to work in the world.

FLUIDITY OF CALLING

The church is called to be flexible and brave enough to change with the movement of God in the world. It is easy to stay in our ruts, yet God's call on our lives is fluid. Times and society alter, new communication tools develop, and, of course, people change. The challenge is to remain faithful to the call to serve God and also to be flexible enough to respond to the changing world. We live at a time when change comes fast. The church has not traditionally had the ability to keep pace with moderate change, much less with the pace of change in the modern world. As we grow in our understanding of God and ourselves, God may call us to a different task in order to expand the realm of influence of God's church.

From the times of the biblical record to life in the modern era, God has called people from various careers and moved them into ministry. The new calling does not mean their previous professions were wrong or misguided, and many people do serve God in their professions. It means they began a new season in their lives, and with that change came a new mission and message. Their previous life was not a waste of time, for their earlier life experiences influence the new way they serve God.

The church adapts to the movement of God or it gets left behind. It is essential to remain flexible in understanding God. God is so vast and beyond human understanding that we can easily find ourselves either lost in God's immenseness or tied to our feeble constraints of what we believe God must be. If Amos had not been willing to re-image his life, he probably would have remained in the field with the sheep for the rest of his life. Likewise, without a sense of change in calling, Paul might have remained a Pharisee, Jesus a carpenter, Matthew a tax collector, or Peter a fisherman. While we can serve God as a part of our various professions, God sometimes has something else in mind for us. To be called is to be open to the movement of the Spirit of God in our lives and in the world.

This relates to how the church communicates the gospel. What worked in a particular era may be inadequate for the next. In order for people to hear it, we must interpret the message of the gospel in ways that make sense to the world in which we live. The church is called to share the gospel message, and to be effective, the church has to find meaningful ways for the culture and society to hear and respond to the presence of God in the world. The church needs to be willing to re-image its path and follow God in new directions.

INVOLVING THE WHOLE LIFE

The church is called to involve the entirety of life in the Christian journey. It is easy to compartmentalize our lives to the degree that one area does not interfere with another. It is difficult to balance the demands of work, home, family, community, and church, and along the way people make choices and prioritize their commitments. At times, the church is not the top priority, yet that neither makes one less Christian nor removes one from the responsibility of living a Christian lifestyle. There is a danger in compartmentalizing the world between secular life and sacred life to the degree that we see ourselves as Christians only at church, with little regard to the way we live outside the church. In the world of the twenty-first century, Christians are called to be who God calls them to be wherever they are.

This is not a new concept; it is as old as the struggle between God and humanity to form a meaningful relationship. The Bible and human history are full of examples of people living out the call of God with their whole lives. One example is the writing and life of Hosea. Hosea's life became his message.

> When the LORD first spoke through Hosea, the LORD said to Hosea, "Go, take for yourself a wife of whoredom and have children of whoredom, for the land commits great whoredom by forsaking the LORD." So he went and took Gomer daughter of Diblaim, and she conceived and bore him a son. And the LORD said to him, "Name him Jezreel; for in a little while I will punish the house of Jehu for the blood of Jezreel, and I will put an end to the kingdom of the house of Israel. On that day I will break the bow of Israel in the valley of Jezreel." She conceived again and bore a daughter. Then the LORD said to him, "Name her Lo-ruhamah, for I will no longer have pity on the house of Israel or forgive them. But I will have pity on the house of Judah, and I will save them by the LORD their God; I will not save them by bow, or by sword, or by war, or by horses, or by horsemen." When she had weaned Lo-ruhamah, she conceived and bore a son. Then the LORD said, "Name him Lo-ammi, for you are not my people and I am not your God." (Hos 1:2-8)

God told Hosea to find a prostitute, marry her, and have children with her. Hosea's marriage with Gomer contains a message about Israel forsaking the covenant. In those days Israel was "prostituting" with other gods and turning away from the covenant. God was displeased with their choice of worshiping other gods, and God called Hosea to let the people of Israel know. Hosea and Gomer's entire life was a prophecy, even to the naming of their children. First, Jezreel was born, and his name means "in a little while." In a little while, God would punish the house of Jehu, and Israel would be destroyed. Hosea named the next child Lo-ruhamah, meaning "not pitied," which indicated that God would no longer pity Israel or Judah and would not save them from what was to come. Finally, a third child was named Lo-ammi, "not my people." No longer would Israel be the people of God.

Over and over again, Hosea's life mirrored the relationship and message of God to Israel. Hosea lived out God's message to the people of Israel from his relationship with his wife Gomer to the naming of his children. Each element of Hosea's life became a prophecy to Israel about their falling away from relationship with God and their need to reestablish the relationship by turning back to God. The prophet's writings end with a sign of hope. If Israel returns to the covenant, God will forgive them and work with them to put an end to their prostitution. All is not lost; there is hope.

As we look at the lives of Christians, what message are we telling the world? The Christian life is neither a perfect lifestyle nor a life without the problems every person faces. Realistically, all human beings fail. No one can live without falling short of what God intends. In fact, the church should not try to uphold the Christian lifestyle as living in perfection. Rather, the Christian life is a relationship with God and humanity that struggles to bind and build the connection. As that relationship develops, people live the Christian life in a world that at times looks for the sensational. Christians are called to live a life that portrays the gospel. Out of gratitude toward God's love for us, we return that love toward God and people. The essential question becomes how to live into that relationship and, in the process of living it, show the world the presence of God in life and in the world.

Today people run the risk of becoming isolated and living only within their cubicles. Yet the explosion of social networking communities where people can share personal experiences yields hope in the continuing human need for community. Social networking is not a traditional way of understanding human community, but it demonstrates the human desire to be in relationship. Christians are not solo entities without support or community. While you can be a Christian on the golf course, the golf course may not bring you Christian community. We need community, and we also need to understand that the Christian community is not the only place where the Christian should be. We must seek a balance between living securely in the nurturing community and living the Christian life in the world.

Hosea did not keep to himself; the nation of Israel during his life might have appreciated it if he had. However, for the community of Israel, Hosea presented a message of judgment and eventual hope. Out of the Christian community, Christians go to proclaim the message of grace and hope in Jesus Christ. We are nurtured in the message through community, and then we proclaim the message through the ways we live. The Christian message involves our whole lives, not only our Sunday selves.

A SURPRISING CALLING

God's calling is surprising. God often calls unexpected individuals. In the Bible, God seems to choose the least prepared. God called Abraham, childless and old, to be the father of a great nation whose descendants would be as numerous as grains of sand. God called Moses, a self-professed stutterer who fled Egypt after murdering an Egyptian, to go before Pharaoh and ask for the release of Israel. God called David, the youngest son of Jesse from the smallest tribe of Israel, to become a great king. God came as a carpenter and a suffering servant to invite humanity into relationship. Perhaps God calls the least likely people to show that, ultimately, life and creation belong to God. Human pride and arrogance can quickly set in when we think we have the skills to tackle a task. Only when we recognize human limits can we truly invite God to do marvelous things. It is surprising to see *whom* God calls to ministry.

It is also surprising *how* God calls. God does not use just one type of event. God has a way of surprising us when we least expect it, and the call of God does not always occur at the most religious places. God came to Gideon as he threshed wheat in a wine press. God interrupted Paul on his way to persecute Christians in Damascus. God calls people as they live their ordinary lives, sometimes with little expectation that God would call them. Noah was going about his life when God called him to build an ark. Amos was among the shepherds at Tekoa when God called him to be a prophet. Peter was working in his family's fishing business when Jesus called him to be a disciple. James was mending nets when Jesus called him to be a disciple. Similar examples abound in Scripture. There are also times when God comes into a holy place to call people, such as Isaiah in the temple in Jerusalem or Moses on the mountain of God.

Let us reflect further on this aspect of God's reaching out to humanity. The twelve disciples of Jesus were all called from one life to another. Peter had a family fishing business when he met Jesus. In the Gospel of Matthew, we find this story of the call of Peter, Andrew, James, and John:

> As he walked by the Sea of Galilee, he saw two brothers, Simon, who is called Peter, and Andrew his brother, casting a net into the lake—for they were fishermen. And he said to them, "Follow me, and I will make you fish for people." Immediately they left their nets and followed him. As he went from there, he saw two other brothers, James son of Zebedee and his brother John, in the boat with their father Zebedee, mending their nets, and he called them. Immediately they left the boat and their father, and followed him. (Matt 4:18-22)

What would cause someone to drop what he or she was doing and follow another person? It is surprising that these men simply dropped their nets without any knowledge of Jesus or his mission, and we can speculate as to whether they knew Jesus before he approached them. However, that does not seem to be as important as their response to the call of Jesus to follow him. They went, seemingly with little or no understanding of what lay ahead for them. The call of God surprises us, and the results of that call are often surprising as well. No one can anticipate the future, nor can anyone have a full understanding of what the Christian life will bring. Humanity simply follows God into an unknown future, certain only of God's constant, loving presence.

Paul's conversion experience was certainly one of great surprise, both to Paul and to the early Christian community. On his way to Damascus to bring followers of the "Way" back to Jerusalem, Saul, as he was originally known, saw "a light from heaven."

> He fell to the ground and heard a voice saying to him, "Saul, Saul, why do you persecute me?" He asked, "Who

are you, Lord?" The reply came, "I am Jesus, whom you are persecuting. But get up and enter the city, and you will be told what you are to do." The men who were traveling with him stood speechless because they heard the voice but saw no one. Saul got up from the ground, and though his eyes were open, he could see nothing; so they led him by the hand and brought him into Damascus. For three days he was without sight, and neither ate nor drank.

Now there was a disciple in Damascus named Ananias. The Lord said to him in a vision, "Ananias." He answered, "Here I am, Lord." The Lord said to him, "Get up and go to the street called Straight, and at the house of Judas look for a man of Tarsus named Saul. At this moment he is praying, and he has seen in a vision a man named Ananias come in and lay his hands on him so that he might regain his sight." But Ananias answered, "Lord, I have heard from many about this man, how much evil he has done to your saints in Jerusalem; and here he has authority from the chief priests to bind all who invoke your name." But the Lord said to him, "Go, for he is an instrument whom I have chosen to bring my name before Gentiles and kings and before the people of Israel; I myself will show him how much he must suffer for the sake of my name." So Ananias went and entered the house. He laid his hands on Saul and said, "Brother Saul, the Lord Jesus, who appeared to you on your way here, has sent me so that you may regain your sight and be filled with the Holy Spirit." And immediately something like scales fell from his eyes, and his sight was restored. Then he got up and was baptized, and after taking some food, he regained his strength. (Acts 9:4-19)

Saul was the great defender of the Jewish faith in the face of the growing Christian population. Both Jews and

Christians knew him and his mission to stop the Christian movement. After the stoning of Stephen, the followers of Jesus left Jerusalem and scattered all around the ancient world, and with them went the gospel message, spreading around the world because of the actions of those who wanted to end the movement. Saul must have gotten word about a group in Damascus and received permission to go and bring them to Jerusalem for trial. He was stopped only by a divine revelation from God, which left him blinded and confused. Those traveling with him took him on to Damascus, where Paul spent time reflecting on the experience through prayer and fasting.

The surprise was not only for Saul, but for Ananias as well. There is little doubt that Ananias was surprised by his vision, and possibly he even questioned what he thought he heard. After all, he knew about Saul and seemed aware of Saul's mission. Why would Ananias want to get involved in such a dangerous situation? It would make Saul's job easier. Yet the surprises continued as Ananias went to Saul. The hunted became the one through whom God worked to convert the hunter into the essence of that which he hunted. There is irony here. Saul hunted Christians, and when he found them he was transformed from hunter to hunted. God surprises us by choosing the one no one would expect to accomplish God's purposes in the world. Only a God of surprises would bother to change the heart of the one breathing hatred toward the Christian church so that he would become one of the greatest evangelists the church has ever known.

The church is a called community. Responding to the call of God is part of the culture of the church. Calling requires a radical change in our lives if we are to invite people to intersect their life journeys with God's ever-expanding relationship with creation. Christianity calls for our entire lives, not only our Sunday selves. The United Methodist communion liturgy puts it this way: "Pour out your Holy Spirit on us gathered here, and on these gifts of bread and wine. Make them be for us the body and blood of Christ, that we may be for the world the body of Christ, redeemed by his blood."[1]

The church tells the story of God's reaching out to creation through the everyday lives of God's followers, wherever they find themselves. The church knows the living story of the grace of a living God. God calls the church to go into the world in ever-changing ways to share the message of the gospel of Jesus Christ by connecting the story of each life with the story of God's relationship with the world. What does that gospel mean? What are we communicating to a world that seeks meaning and community? We will now explore the content of the surprising story of God's love to the entire world.

NOTE

1. *The United Methodist Book of Worship* (Nashville: United Methodist Publishing House: 1992) 38.

Chapter 2

I LOVE TO TELL THE STORY

When people think of the church, what message do they hear? Various messages claim to be gospel, and some even contradict one another. God's story is multi-faceted and involves many different times, places, and people. Again, the story of the church is not its own; the church did not create the story, but it communicates the story. To understand the story, one starts with the Bible and works from there into each individual life. Let us begin with the biblical message to seek new insights and understandings of God's story with humanity.

The Nicodemus story in the Gospel of John concludes with one of the most cited passages in the Bible. One cannot go to a sporting event without seeing it on a poster board: "For God so loved the world that he gave his only Son, so that everyone who believes in him may not perish but may have eternal life" (John 3:16). We tend to stop there, believing that is the complete story, but the next verses expand it.

Indeed, God did not send the Son into the world to condemn the world, but in order that the world might be saved through him. Those who believe in him are not condemned; but those who do not believe are condemned already, because they have not believed in the name of the only Son of God. And this is the judgment, that the light has come into the world, and people loved darkness rather than light because their deeds were evil. For all who do evil hate the light and do not come to the light, so that their deeds may not be exposed. But those who do what is true come to the light, so that it may be clearly seen that their deeds have been done in God. (John 3:17-21)

It is essential to understand that Jesus did not come to condemn humanity. Humanity continues to separate from God, but Jesus came to offer another way. Jesus preached a message focused on building relationships with God and healing relationships with people. He came to declare that the Reign of God was near. With the advent of Christ, the world changed. The message of the church is about God's sending Jesus into the world with a message of hope and healing.

Often we hear messages either of doom and despair or of prosperity and riches. Neither message presents the gospel message in a healthy way to a hurting world. Proclaiming a message of condemnation tends to scare people or turn them off. Preaching a message of material riches as a reward for following God becomes shallow when life's realities bring difficult times. The message of the Reign of God coming near is one of hope to the entire human race. We have separated ourselves from God, so what can we do? What does one tell a condemned person? What words of comfort and grace apply as we examine life? John recognizes the trait in human beings to prefer darkness to light. Does it help to continue to point out people's failures without offering a lifeline?

The message of hope and grace shines the light of God into our lives and shows us the dark corners that need transforming. As we communicate the gospel, there is no need to condemn others. As each person begins to experience grace, God shows him or her what lurks within the dark places of the human soul. Grace starts with humanity where we are, and it does not leave us there. We do nothing to bring grace into our lives, but once it covers us, grace changes us. Though grace is offered to us without price, grace is always costly. Dietrich Bonhoeffer, a German theologian who lived during World War II and eventually died opposing Hitler, puts it this way: "It is grace because God did not reckon his Son too dear a price to pay for our life, but delivered him up for us. Costly grace is the Incarnation of God."[1]

Grace is also transformative; it refines us by removing the things in our lives that keep us from relationship with God and with one another. This is not a once and forever ideal. We are always in process, always in need of grace, always re-created. Grace is not about being without faults and sin; rather, it is about learning to recognize them and moving closer to God in the midst of temptation.

Paul's letter to the Romans helps us gain a deeper appreciation of what God has done:

> For while we were still weak, at the right time Christ died for the ungodly. Indeed, rarely will anyone die for a righteous person—though perhaps for a good person someone might actually dare to die. But God proves his love for us in that while we still were sinners Christ died for us. Much more surely then, now that we have been justified

> by his blood, will we be saved through him from the
> wrath of God. For if while we were enemies, we were rec-
> onciled to God through the death of his Son, much more
> surely, having been reconciled, will we be saved by his
> life. But more than that, we even boast in God through
> our Lord Jesus Christ, through whom we have now
> received reconciliation. (Rom 5:6-11)

God became incarnate while humanity was still out of sync
with God. God did not wait to enter the world until
humanity was able to fully understand the need; rather, God
came into human history while humanity was separated
from God. God starts where we are and encourages us to be
transformed. The story the church shares will shake the
world to its core as it calls the entire cosmos into relationship with the Creator. In the writing of Romans, Paul uses
the images of Adam and Christ to reflect on God's gift to the
world in the incarnation.

> Therefore, just as sin came into the world through one
> man, and death came through sin, and so death spread to
> all because all have sinned— sin was indeed in the world
> before the law, but sin is not reckoned when there is no
> law. Yet death exercised dominion from Adam to Moses,
> even over those whose sins were not like the transgression
> of Adam, who is a type of the one who was to come. But
> the free gift is not like the trespass. For if the many died
> through the one man's trespass, much more surely have
> the grace of God and the free gift in the grace of the one
> man, Jesus Christ, abounded for the many. And the free
> gift is not like the effect of the one man's sin. For the
> judgment following one trespass brought condemnation,
> but the free gift following many trespasses brings justifi-
> cation. If, because of the one man's trespass, death

exercised dominion through that one, much more surely will those who receive the abundance of grace and the free gift of righteousness exercise dominion in life through the one man, Jesus Christ. Therefore just as one man's trespass led to condemnation for all, so one man's act of righteousness leads to justification and life for all. For just as by the one man's disobedience the many were made sinners, so by the one man's obedience the many will be made righteous. But law came in, with the result that the trespass multiplied; but where sin increased, grace abounded all the more, so that, just as sin exercised dominion in death, so grace might also exercise domin-ion through justification leading to eternal life through Jesus Christ our Lord. (Rom 5:12-21)

One man brings death, one man brings life; one man brings separation, one man brings relationship; one man brings condemnation, one man brings reconciliation. God declared the possibility of a restored relationship through the Incarnation. God broke into history to reclaim creation and begin a process of correction. The church is not perfect in all it does; in fact, the church often struggles to understand God's call. Rather than touting perfection and treating the world in a condescending way, the church is called to see itself in the light of Christ. Within that light, we see how lost we are. That light calls us toward change that brings our life's journey into a vital connection with God.

Sin and separation are part of humanity's common story with God, one another, and the cosmos. While alienation is not the purpose of creation, it is part of the reality in which we live. However, it is not the last chapter of the story. God is in the process of re-creating, and in Jesus God became part of the created order to share grace. Grace brings us into relationship with God and continues to transform humanity back into that for which we were created.

The message of the church is one of life, not death. The church is called to live and share this grace-filled message of life in everything it does. The early church's message is important to hear at this point. This message comes through the millennia and helps us understand what the early church communicated to people. Acts records the first action of the apostles at Pentecost as the beginning of the transformation. In Acts 2:14-36, Peter stands before the people with the rest of the eleven disciples and reminds them of words from the past. Spoken by the prophets Joel and David, these words apply to the life, death, and resurrection of Jesus Christ, insisting that God will save those who call on the name of the Lord and that death is not final. Peter finishes by saying, "Therefore let the entire house of Israel know with certainty that God has made him both Lord and Messiah, this Jesus whom you crucified." His words greatly move those in the early church.

> Now when they heard this, they were cut to the heart and said to Peter and to the other apostles, "Brothers, what should we do?" Peter said to them, "Repent, and be baptized every one of you in the name of Jesus Christ so that your sins may be forgiven; and you will receive the gift of the Holy Spirit. For the promise is for you, for your children, and for all who are far away, everyone whom the Lord our God calls to him." And he testified with many other arguments and exhorted them, saying, "Save yourselves from this corrupt generation." So those who welcomed his message were baptized, and that day about three thousand persons were added. They devoted themselves to the apostles' teaching and fellowship, to the breaking of bread and the prayers. (Acts 2:37-42)

This sermon by Peter retells the salvation history of the world. God had worked this plan of reconciliation from the moment when humanity decided to turn away from God. That is the message of the church, a message of God coming to the world. God works in the hearts of human beings to inspire a longing for what we do not have. Humans cannot change the hearts of people; all we can do is share the story and create the opportunity for God to work. When that happens, they will cry out like those in Acts, "What must we do?" At that point, we show them the path of repentance and belief in the gospel. The story of what God has done leads someone to the discovery that life does not have to be as it is, for God can create something new. Grace is always invitational, calling us away from what we want to what God envisions. We may not always know what God's vision may look like, and so we are often drawn down paths that we would not otherwise choose for ourselves. With God's grace acting in our lives, we never know where God will lead. It starts with the invitation to come back into relationship with God.

The church invites, and God saves! We cannot confuse the two. Otherwise, we raise ourselves to a position of knowing who is invited into the Reign of God and who is excluded from it. The church does not have exclusive rights to decide who receives the invitation to be in the kingdom. The Realm of God is God's alone; the church is the recipient of God's gracious invitation.

The Reign of God is not about numbers or having the most impressive knowledge. It is not about status or human accomplishment. Rather, it is about growing into a relationship that begins here and extends into eternity. Brueggemann writes,

> Evangelism is related to church growth, related but in no
> way synonymous. In speaking of evangelism, one must
> speak of church growth, but only at the end of the dra-
> matic process, and not any sooner. Evangelism is never
> aimed at institutional enhancement or aggrandizement.
> It is aimed simply and solely at summoning people to
> new, liberated obedience to the true governor of all cre-
> ated reality.[2]

The church invites people into relationship with God and the church because of the gracious invitation of God to all humanity. The invitation is not about getting more people to church; at its base, the invitation is to meet God in the midst of life. Evangelism introduces the presence of grace as a reality that exists in all life, and it is the grace of God that initiates the relationship.

The church can easily divert from its message. The message of the church is the old story of the incarnation of Jesus, but many other stories can usurp the main story. Local church traditions often become more important than the gospel. Sometimes the ritual busyness of the church, the traditional events that are continuously held because we have always done it a certain way, distract rather than drive forward the mission of the church. When events or tools become more important than the Realm of God itself, it is time to re-image the vision of the church.

Technology can play a role in the diversion of the church from announcing the nearness of the Realm of God. It is easy to become overly fascinated by the glitz of technology and allow it to become the focal point of the church. Churches add LCDs to their ceilings and pull-down screens in sanctuaries and fellowship halls, sometimes with little thought about how to use these tools to proclaim the Reign of God. Some insist that, since the church down the road has one, we must keep up to date as well. This is not a good use of technology in sharing the story.

Technology is a tool, not the focal point. The church must maintain the balance of keeping the mission of the church true to its calling. Rather than spontaneously ordering the latest and greatest technology off the Internet, the church needs to begin by asking, "What are we going to do with it? How will it help our church tell the story of the Incarnation and saving grace of God?" A church with a focus on the nearness of the Realm of God starts by addressing the purpose of the tool rather than buying a tool and figuring out how to use it later.

The church's mission is already proclaimed. The challenge is how to tell the story. When we tell the story of God's coming into human history with power and conviction, God does wondrous things. The writer of Acts describes the community of faith perhaps at its best:

> Awe came upon everyone, because many wonders and signs were being done by the apostles. All who believed were together and had all things in common; they would sell their possessions and goods and distribute the proceeds to all, as any had need. Day by day, as they spent much time together in the temple, they broke bread at home and ate their food with glad and generous hearts, praising God and having the goodwill of all the people. And day by day the Lord added to their number those who were being saved. (Acts 2:43-47)

Imagine a church where God does signs and wonders, where people support each other, where technology is used as a tool to proclaim the story in powerful ways, where praising God and serving humanity is of the utmost importance in the community. Imagine a church where God's story is told so that people hear it and understand it, and where God is allowed room to move within a person's life. To tell the story of God's reaching out to humankind is to participate in the awesome experience of God's coming in a real way to the world. It is to be willing to step aside and let God work to transform all humankind. It is about inviting people to be part of the community of faith, where God can work to transform all humanity, including us. It's not about anyone other than God. Paul shares his thoughts on how to tell the story:

> When I came to you, brothers and sisters, I did not come proclaiming the mystery of God to you in lofty words or wisdom. For I decided to know nothing among you except Jesus Christ, and him crucified. And I came to you in weakness and in fear and in much trembling. My speech and my proclamation were not with plausible words of wisdom, but with a demonstration of the Spirit and of power, so that your faith might rest not on human wisdom but on the power of God. (1 Cor 2:1-5)

The church must remain focused on telling the story. We must utilize technology as a tool to tell the story. It is easy to look upon the church as the end of the mission rather than the mission itself. When this happens, the church becomes concerned about how many new members it acquires, how many people attend weekly, the superiority of its technology, or the size of its budget or staff. When the church understands itself as the teller of the story and God as the instigator of change, then the focus moves to how the story is told rather than how many people respond.

The teller of the story does not depend on how the hearer receives the story. The church is called to tell the story. It is God's role to take the efforts of the church and expand it into the world in ways that bring change and transformation. Humans are limited, but God uses human effort. We must remember to give God the glory for what comes. Evangelism is not salvation; rather, God's actions in the past and present bring salvation and ultimately conform the cosmos to the purpose God intended.

The church and the Reign of God are about God at work. The gospel proclaimed through the church is formed and transmitted through us, but God is still the primary actor who transforms human life and history. The gospel does not depend on the church, but the church does depend on the gospel to continue to transform the community of faith. The church itself is invited into the story to share it with the world. As Brueggemann wrote,

> Resurrection faith with its cosmic claims, leads to an active practice of generosity and compassion, surely the Lord's own work that is to be done by the community that receives the news. . . . The church is empowered for transformed life in the world, authorized to act counter to the ways of the world. In sum, the community which hears the news is invited to a life of hospitality as a way to counter a world bent on vengeance.[3]

The church that lives into the story is often counter-cultural. The message of the gospel is different from the message of culture. God's message ultimately confronts the world's story and eventually overcomes it. The story of the gospel is not easy to share, for it brings the teller into conflict with powers, people, and the ways of the world. The story the church tells transforms life because the story is ultimately God moving in the cosmos to effect change; human beings and human culture tend to reject change.

The story of God's grace is not easy to tell, nor always sweet to hear. It challenges us to put ourselves into the back seat and let God take control. It is always in need of being re-communicated in ways that the contemporary world can understand. It invites us into a transforming relationship with a surprising God who will move us into areas where we do not want to go. It confronts humanity with the reality that human beings are not in control of the destiny of the cosmos. Instead, God shines from the story to declare God's control and power to do God's will to accomplish God's purpose.

NOTES

1. Dietrich Bonhoeffer, *The Cost of Discipleship*, trans. R.H. Fuller (New York: Macmillan Publishing Company, 1963) 48.

2. Walter Brueggemann, *Biblical Perspectives on Evangelism: Living in a Three Storied Universe* (Nashville: Abingdon Press, 1993) 45.

3. Ibid., 36.

Chapter 3

TO ALL THE WORLD

The church is called to share a message of good news. It seems simplistic to say the church is to tell the story to everyone, and yet that is the call. Does the church decide to whom to communicate the gospel? If so, what are the criteria? Must people be of the right moral character or perhaps the right race or nationality in order to hear the gospel? The message is not the church's to manipulate. The message of the nearness of the Realm of God is God's to deliver; the church is simply one mechanism through which God chooses to operate.

Multiple groups are invited to hear the message of the nearness of God. The most obvious are people outside the church religiously, culturally, or economically. Some people do not know about the good news of God's incarnation in Jesus Christ. Some are oblivious to the presence of God in their midst or have had experiences that created an uneasy feeling about religion of any kind. They need to hear the story of God's grace for them.

However, one cannot overlook the need of the church itself to continue to hear the gospel message. Some people inside the church need to hear again what God has done. The church is an imperfect community, and sometimes incidents occur that turn people away from God. Events will occur that are outside the realm of Christian community. Sometimes it feels like where two or more are gathered, there will be conflict! When this happens, people get confused and need to experience the story of grace again. Thank God that Jesus promises to be there too! Those inside the church need to hear the story in order to come back to God continually. When people lose sight of God, they need the church to help them refocus on the gospel. Forgetting the gospel message can easily cause the church to become another social or activist organization. People need to hear the gospel for different reasons, and different forms of communication are often necessary. Right now we will concern ourselves with the various groupings and the variety of their needs. Later, we will explore the tools needed to reach out to the groups.

WITHIN THE FAMILY

What if the family does not know the story? Families have marvelous stories about the good and bad times that bind them together. To forget the stories is to lose one's identity as a part of the family. There are vacation stories of fun and humorous times relaxing together, or tales of troubled times when solutions seemed evasive. All of these experiences make up the family life and give each individual an identity within the family.

The church is a family, and its stories function in the same way. Each congregation has unique stories that make up its identity. There are humorous tales as well as hardships the community has endured. Above all, though, is the one story that unites all Christian congregations and denominations together, and that is the incarnation story of God breaking into human history. A church that has forgotten the gospel message of the nearness of the Reign of God runs the danger of losing its identity.

The church must continue to hear the story. From the pulpit, from lives lived in the world, and from study, people within Christian congregations have a need to be challenged in Christian discipleship. Such growth in understanding of each other's particular place within the modern chapters of God's story keeps the church from straying away from God's call. The church community is called to discover its unique calling within God's Reign. The church must grow in its discipleship in response to God's gracious invitation.

There are also times in human life that bring spiritual turmoil and doubt. None of us are spiritual giants in all situations. Doubting and difficult times are part of human life, and being a church member does not stop such negative events from happening; in fact, sometimes events within the church cause people to have doubts and lose faith. However, the gospel message speaks a word of hope to humanity's times of doubts. Unless we are continually exposed to that gospel word, times of doubts and trouble can overwhelm us. The church is called to share the message again and again with those who have already heard and responded to it in order to maintain the Christian identity that God works to develop in each person.

Becoming a part of the church is not the end. Rather, to commit oneself to the church is to commit oneself to a life of growth and development as a Christian person. The gospel message is a continual presence in life and challenges the way we live. Without that continual growth, life can stagnate and cause a loss of understanding and identity. The story informs Christians of who they are, and without the story there is a danger of forgetting our Christian identity.

IT'S A SMALL WORLD AFTER ALL

Proclaiming the gospel message cannot cease at the inner walls of the church; the church is called to go into the world. People who are outside the life of the church exist in a variety of settings—different religious practices, economic situations, cultures, and languages. Each has a unique set of circumstances and possibilities. The technological advances of our world bring the human family into close contact with one another, perhaps more so than at any time in history. How does one communicate the gospel justly in such a multi-cultural, multi-religious world?

Cultural and Religious Differences

In earlier times in the United States, life seemed easier and simpler. Communities were fairly homogeneous, and the sight of someone outside the norm of a particular area tended to bring skepticism and mistrust. Technology has changed the structure of human society. No longer do most humans live next to people who look like them or believe like them. With the advances in technology and communication, we may live among people of a different nationality, race, or religion. Communities are also confronted online with a variety of ideas and thoughts, both religiously and culturally. Our exposure to human experience continues to expand as technology creates new areas of contact in the human family. As technology makes our world smaller, we are confronted with a number of worldviews and religions.

When our family moved into a new area, we went through the usual struggles, including finding a home. We went to house after house, and soon they begin to blur together: homes spotlessly cleaned with immaculate lawns, all inviting potential buyers to pick them. One house we examined was different from all the others, not because we chose it, but because of what we found there. One room was dedicated to religion. There were candles, an altar, pictures of family, and statues of what I believe were Hindu gods and goddesses. I was intrigued and wanted to linger and gaze upon the elements of the practice of one's faith. But I was also reminded that in society, we cannot assume everyone we meet is of similar background, faith, cultural understandings, or belief systems.

The world is becoming a smaller place as technology brings people together. One can travel on an airplane to anywhere in the world in a matter of hours. People can use the Internet to view areas of the world that they may never visit and in some way experience people and cultures that are alien to their own. On social networking sites, we can read about people of different faiths. We can read "tweets" from Twitter about how different faiths influence another worldview. We go shopping and see the dress and language of many cultures, and perhaps we wonder about the headdress, colorful garments, or other aspects of a culture that may be foreign to us.

What is the result of this infusion of different cultures? Sometimes it is mistrust, and other times it is misunderstanding. Different thought patterns and languages create the possibility of confusion. We rarely make time to learn about different cultures. We are simply forced into contact with one another without the tools necessary to communicate effectively. Then the possibilities of building meaningful relationships decay into trying to make everyone else look and sound like us. Then come hatred and anger as cultures collide into each other to the point where mistrust and misunderstanding become actions of violence and words of separation and hurt.

Technology and communication tools bring our world together, while culture and religion threaten to rip it apart. How does the church communicate the gospel message in the diversity of modern society without judgment or condemnation of humanity and culture? Scott Jones offers insight into loving people who are not like "us":

> If evangelism is based primarily on God's universal love for all humanity, it surely follows that such love includes respect for others' beliefs and practices. Truly loving others means knowing them and understanding who they are and why they live the way they do. It means understanding their culture and learning its internal logic so that its relation to the gospel of Jesus Christ can be made clear.[1]

The church is called to share good news, not to condemn or belittle others for their culture and religious actions. In terms of technology, the church is called to understand it and use it as appropriate to share the gospel. By learning about Facebook, Twitter, and other types of community technology, the church can begin to explore new ways of expressing the gospel message. Sharing the good news with people of other faiths and cultures is not about expressing a position of superiority and pompousness. It is about loving people as they are so that they can experience the love of God in their lives.

How can humanity live together in the midst of great diversity? There are no easy answers. Suffice it to say that the church is not the good news but the bearer of Good News. The church is not the salvation of the world but one of the ways God reaches out to the world. Scott Jones helps define the starting point for evangelism to people of non-Christian faiths: "God's mission is to save the world from sin and evil and to re-create it according to God's intention. John 3:16 affirms that God so loved the whole world that the Son was sent to save it and not to condemn it. Thus, any approach to non-Christians must begin with love."[2]

He goes on to describe the atrocities the church committed during the crusades, the inquisition, the conquistadors, and Christian participation in the slave trade all in the name of evangelism and conversion. The church's role is not to convert people forcibly to the Christian faith, even if that could be done. The church's role is not to scare people into some sort of faith response that will not stand the test of time and trouble. The church's role is to love people by sharing the story of God's reaching out into human history to offer hope and grace to people of all nations. As the world draws closer together through technological advances, and as cultures intermix, the church is called to the task of sharing good news of great joy. It is news of God's love for all God's creation. God touches the human heart and assists humanity in experiencing a relationship with God.

A story in the Bible depicts Jesus' disciples as being upset because someone who was not a part of their group cast out demons in Jesus' name. The disciples told the man to stop, but Jesus chastised them, saying, "Do not stop him; for whoever is not against you is for you" (Luke 9:50). Is it not possible that God works in ways the church cannot comprehend or understand? Before Christians judge people too quickly, perhaps we need to pause and try to gain understanding of unfamiliar people and religions. Perhaps it is important for the church to show humility and be welcoming and hospitable to all people. Jesus shared his understanding of what it meant to welcome people:

> An argument arose among them as to which one of them was the greatest. But Jesus, aware of their inner thoughts, took a little child and put it by his side, and said to them, "Whoever welcomes this child in my name welcomes me, and whoever welcomes me welcomes the one who sent me; for the least among all of you is the greatest." (Luke 9:46-48)

To welcome others is to show them love and acceptance just as they are. It is not to try to change them into an image to which we think they must conform. The church is called to love all God's children by building a relationship whereby each individual's story is heard and the gospel story proclaimed as a reality that intersects their story. For God is at work in all of creation in ways the human mind cannot comprehend. The church is called to share the story in a relationship of love, knowing that it is God's story to develop in any way God chooses. As a part of that great story of God reaching out into the world, the church shares its part of God's wonderful tapestry.

ECONOMIC DIFFERENCES

The economics of computer and technology access is important to keep in mind. As the church explores using technology, there is a danger in excluding people with low income who have no access to the Internet. In the United States, a racial and economic divide exists around technology. Some enjoy easy access to modern technology, and some do not. This divide need not pose a stumbling block to the church's use of technology. Creative ministries can offer an opportunity for people who cannot afford personal computers to access them through the church. Providing computer access might even pave the road for an individual to have better employment opportunities.

We can see the technology gap. Some individuals and families simply cannot afford computers and/or Internet service. Those in this situation quickly get left behind in many areas, including education and lifestyle, but hopefully not religion. The church cannot get so caught up in the technological age that it forgets the poor. Sharing the story is not only for those who have money and influence and therefore access to technology; it is also for those without such means.

To communicate effectively to the poor, the church must use multiple platforms for reaching out. One method is the tried and true print media. The postal service delivers into areas where technology may not reach. Brochures, flyers, posters, and other types of invitational materials can advertise specific areas or events at the church. Perhaps the church can reach out by inviting the poor for special worship services, meals at special times, or the like.

The effort to reach out cannot stop with print or with any technology. At its foundation, sharing the Christian faith is *relational.* The church's call to proclaim good news often involves forming relationships with people who are not necessarily like "us." It is not always easy to be a church community that invites people who are different from us, yet the call of God to share the nearness of the Reign of God is at times uncomfortable. The nearness of God is for all people, as the angel announced long ago to a group of tired and dirty shepherds: "Do not be afraid; for see—I am bringing you good news of great joy for all the people: to you is born this day in the city of David a Savior, who is the Messiah, the Lord" (Luke 2:10b-11). I've heard preachers try to clean up that story by saying these were special shepherds responsible for sheep used in the temple and thus understood the birth of the Messiah better than poor, simple shepherds. But trying to make the shepherds more acceptable to us is giving Luke's Gospel a bath! The announcement of the coming of God into the world in an unexpected way comes to the most unexpected people—the poor and culturally outcast. Over and over again, Luke's Gospel declares God's grace to the marginalized of society.

MOSAIC OUTREACH

God's Reign is a mosaic full of color, culture, and thought. It is an invitation to share beliefs, stories, traditions, and life and to understand and relate to one another. God's Reign is not about condemning people, but learning from one another; it is created out of God's incarnation into human history and the invitation is God's to give. Each Christian has a role to play in extending the invitation and working to communicate the gospel message in meaningful ways.

The gift of technology is bringing the world together in unprecedented ways economically, culturally, and linguistically. The human capacity to define differences between people and build walls threatens to rip the world apart. In the midst of this ever-changing world, the church is called to share the message of the gospel with all people. To accomplish this task fully, the church must look closely at those with whom the church communicates. How homogeneous is the church community? How does it reflect the community around the church building?

As Paul wrote to the churches in the city of Corinth, he considered what was necessary to communicate the gospel to a diverse community. His answer was to approach people within their cultural and social station.

> If I proclaim the gospel, this gives me no ground for boasting, for an obligation is laid on me, and woe to me if I do not proclaim the gospel! For if I do this of my own will, I have a reward; but if not of my own will, I am entrusted with a commission. What then is my reward? Just this: that in my proclamation I may make the gospel free of charge, so as not to make full use of my rights in the gospel. For though I am free with respect to all, I have made myself a slave to all, so that I might win more of them. To the Jews I became as a Jew, in order to win Jews. To those under the law I became as one under the law (though I myself am not under the law) so that I might win those under the law. To those outside the law I became as one outside the law (though I am not free from God's law but am under Christ's law) so that I might win those outside the law. To the weak I became weak, so that I might win the weak. I have become all things to all people, that I might by all means save some. I do it all for the sake of the gospel, so that I may share in its blessings. (1 Cor 9:16-23)

At first glance Paul seems hypocritical, as he is willing to change depending on his audience. People often behave one way with a certain group of people and change their behavior with another group. People also frequently try to avoid conflict by living their lives in particular ways with particular people in order to make everyone happy. However, Paul is not a people pleaser, and we know from his letters that there are times when he stands in the middle of conflict. When conflict finds him, Paul does not shrink from it but confronts it. Paul's goal is not to make people happy; rather, his goal is to please God in all that he does.

Paul was under no delusion; God put on his heart the task of taking the gospel to the world. It is a message and a mission that he did not choose; God chose it for him. Paul carried out God's mission using whatever means lay at his disposal to tell everyone he could reach the gospel message.

Paul's approach was relational. He presented the gospel in a way that all people could hear. He did not condemn or approach people with an air of superiority. Instead, he related with people where they were so that they might hear the gospel. His mission went beyond a benefit for himself. He had a message to proclaim. For the sake of the gospel, Paul became all things for all people. Paul would do anything to reach out to others with the gospel message. His prime motivation was the proclamation of the gospel by whatever means necessary. That understanding of his mission led him to travel to faraway places, suffer insults and beatings, and endure life in prison. Church tradition tells us that Paul ultimately gave up his life to proclaim the gospel.

In this multicultural world, the church is called to reach out to all people in whatever ways are necessary to communicate the gospel. All are invited to be a part of the church community, but first they must understand the invitation. Numerous tools are available for the church to use in proclaiming the gospel message. Throughout history, the church has been able to adapt the gospel so that it relates to the people and society that surrounds it. This is always the church's challenge: to adapt so that the message of the gospel is understood without changing the gospel itself. In the next chapter, we explore ways the church has proclaimed the gospel message in an effort to search for trends and methods that can be used in today's social, cultural, and religious reality. By studying the past, we can stand on the shoulders of those who preceded this generation and recognize the ways they addressed society's changing needs.

NOTES

1. Scott Jones, *The Evangelistic Love of God and Neighbor* (Nashville: Abingdon Press, 2003) 163.

2. Ibid., 162.

Chapter 4

TOOLS FOR COMMUNICATING: WHAT HAS THE CHURCH DONE?

The church is called to tell a story that it did not create in order to offer a relationship with God that only God can establish. That is the church's theological and real-world task. How is the church to perform this task? To share the story with power, the church is called to crawl out of the ruts of preexisting fashions and methods. God is constantly on the move, and the story does not stand still. Instead, it is continually revealed to all God's people. God tells the story in new ways with the available tools. God has provided the tools to accomplish the communication of the gospel, and the church must meet the challenge of choosing which tools to use and deciding how to use them.

For many years, the church has used certain comfortable tools. We tend to turn to them first, using them with vigor.

We can see what these tools once did for the church, and we sometimes wonder why they don't work as well today. The church often becomes stuck in the memory of its own past, and getting out of that rut is difficult. People don't like to change their utensils and methodology. "We have always done it that way!" some protest. "We did it this way before I was born and while I was growing up. It was fine then, and it is fine now." How often we hear those voices in churches whose pews are empty on Sunday, whose Sunday school rooms lie dormant, and whose filmstrips lie dusty in a closet!

How does the church communicate effectively in a world where communication has changed rapidly from telephone to high-speed Internet? In the nearly 135 years since the telephone was patented in 1876, the world of communications has changed greatly. Most of that change has come within the last few decades with the growth of computer use, the Internet, and email. While people living in Bible times certainly did not have these tools, we can learn something from how people communicated in the past. Our spiritual ancestors used every means at their disposal to share with the world the message of God's grace. These ancestors of the church can help us learn not to fear using the new tools God has provided, even if it means updating how we proclaim the story. By looking at how the church communicated in the past, we can discover general themes and characteristics of the tools that may help us pick up new tools today with more confidence.

FAMILIAR ELEMENTS

The church has consistently used common, familiar elements of culture and society that people are accustomed to seeing and using. By means of recognizable elements of life such as common practice and common household or work items, church leaders have been able to talk about humanity's relationship with God. Jesus and his disciples used experiences well known to the people of their day to illustrate truths about the Reign of God. Today some of these practices seem odd, but to people of Jesus' day they were ordinary, everyday experiences. To fully understand them, it is essential to study ancient practices. Already it is evident that limitations exist to using familiar elements of culture and society. Society changes, and the memorable associations of culture change, so the methods of telling the story of God must change. This calls the church to take the time to fully explore such elements of the past, not to replicate the specific tools that were used, but to understand how they were used so that we can apply the methodology today.

To begin, Jesus used examples from the world around him to communicate the fact that the Reign of God had come near to establish a relationship with humanity like people had never before known. Jesus spoke differently than many of the religious leaders; he inspired and fascinated people. By using familiar elements of life, he showed people God's love for them and demonstrated that God cared about their struggles. The parables Jesus told were filled with examples of life from first-century Palestine. One in particular demonstrates the point. In this parable Jesus speaks about a sower of seeds.

> "Listen! A sower went out to sow. And as he sowed, some seeds fell on the path, and the birds came and ate them up. Other seeds fell on rocky ground, where they did not have much soil, and they sprang up quickly, since they had no depth of soil. But when the sun rose, they were scorched; and since they had no root, they withered away.

> Other seeds fell among thorns, and the thorns grew up
> and choked them. Other seeds fell on good soil and
> brought forth grain, some a hundredfold, some sixty,
> some thirty. Let anyone with ears listen!" (Matt 13:3b-9)

The people who heard this parable had experienced this type of farming method. They saw farmers planting their crops and understood that some seeds come up and others do not. Our interest here is not so much the interpretation of the parable, but the fact that Jesus frequently used recognizable objects and experiences of people's lives to talk about the Reign of God. Other parables include a woman who searches for a lost coin, a person who finds a treasure in a field, weeds growing in a field of wheat, and many more. People understood and perhaps experienced the illustrations Jesus used. Jesus touched people where they lived, and his familiar packaging of the gospel helped spread the good news.

Jesus also used the news of the day to communicate something about the gospel. This story from the Gospel of Luke shows Jesus' knowledge of world events and how he weaved them into his conversations.

> At that very time there were some present who told him
> about the Galileans whose blood Pilate had mingled with
> their sacrifices. He asked them, "Do you think that
> because these Galileans suffered in this way they were
> worse sinners than all other Galileans? No, I tell you; but
> unless you repent, you will all perish as they did. Or
> those eighteen who were killed when the tower of Siloam
> fell on them—do you think that they were worse offend-
> ers than all the others living in Jerusalem? No, I tell you;
> but unless you repent, you will all perish just as they
> did." (Luke 13:1-5)

In this passage Jesus uses two stories to talk about the need to return to God. Both incidents were fresh on his listeners' minds, and they were likely trying to make sense of them. In the first incident, Pilate killed Galileans who were making sacrifices. In the second, a tower fell, killing innocent people. The first incident is an example of humanity's cruelty to humanity, while the second one relates to the problem of why bad things happen to good people. Jesus was able to use both events to talk about God and communicate to his listeners something about the gospel message. Out of the familiar, and also the horrific, comes an opportunity to share something about the meaning of the gospel. Such teachable moments are always available to the church, and they do not have to be dramatic events as the next story indicates.

In another story, Jesus encounters a teachable moment to communicate the gospel. Here the opportunity arises with a question as opposed to a dramatic incident. It was a question meant to entrap Jesus, but he manages to turn it around on his questioners. Jesus is asked a question about taxes, and his response includes a visual aid and a faith challenge.

> Then the Pharisees went and plotted to entrap him in what he said. So they sent their disciples to him, along with the Herodians, saying, "Teacher, we know that you are sincere, and teach the way of God in accordance with truth, and show deference to no one; for you do not regard people with partiality. Tell us, then, what you think. Is it lawful to pay taxes to the emperor, or not?" But Jesus, aware of their malice, said, "Why are you putting me to the test, you hypocrites? Show me the coin used for the tax." And they brought him a denarius.

Then he said to them, "Whose head is this, and whose
title?" They answered, "The emperor's." Then he said to
them, "Give therefore to the emperor the things that are
the emperor's, and to God the things that are God's."
When they heard this, they were amazed; and they left
him and went away. (Matt 22:15-22)

This passage is full of common elements that Jesus uses
to talk about God. Nearly every human society recognizes
taxes and money. In a letter to Jean-Baptiste Leroy written
November 13, 1789, Benjamin Franklin wrote, "Our new
Constitution is now established, and has an appearance that
promises permanency; but in this world nothing can be said
to be certain except death and taxes."[1] Taxes are an ordinary
part of human existence. However, the question posed to
Jesus raised interesting issues in terms of Jesus' loyalty to
Israel. Jewish and Roman populations of the time hated and
mistrusted each other, and the Pharisees' question is loaded
with possible traps for Jesus. Also, the Pharisees brought the
Herodians with them. The Herodians supported the family
of Herod and were Roman sympathizers. If Jesus stated that
he was against paying taxes, he would have problems with
the civil authorities. If he supported the tax, the people
would turn hostile toward Jesus.

Jesus avoided the traps and instead pronounced something about the Reign of God. Jesus used another familiar
element, a coin, to move the focus to the struggle between
two empires, Rome and heaven. He asked his questioners
about the coin: "Whose head is this, and whose title?" They
answered, "The emperor's." Then he said to them, "Give
therefore to the emperor the things that are the emperor's,
and to God the things that are God's." Jesus avoided a well-
conceived trap and demonstrated how to use an opportunity

to share the gospel message in a powerful way using a teachable moment and well-known objects.

Another example of the church using available elements is evident when Paul traveled to Athens, a center of philosophical thought in the ancient world. The Athenians built altars for many gods, and one altar was dedicated to any unknown gods whom the Athenians had yet to identify. The incident is related to us in Acts and offers an example of Paul starting with people's understanding of life and moving them to a new perspective. The number of idols in the city upset Paul, and he spent time arguing with religious people, philosophers, and anyone who happened to be at the marketplace. Some in the crowd wondered about him and gave him a platform at the Areopagus, a council site, so he could share his views.

Then Paul stood in front of the Areopagus and said, "Athenians, I see how extremely religious you are in every way. For as I went through the city and looked carefully at the objects of your worship, I found among them an altar with the inscription, 'To an unknown god.' What therefore you worship as unknown, this I proclaim to you. The God who made the world and everything in it, he who is Lord of heaven and earth, does not live in shrines made by human hands, nor is he served by human hands, as though he needed anything, since he himself gives to all mortals life and breath and all things. From one ancestor he made all nations to inhabit the whole earth, and he allotted the times of their existence and the boundaries of the places where they would live, so that they would search for God and perhaps grope for him and find him—though indeed he is not far from each one of us. For 'In him we live and move and have

our being'; as even some of your own poets have said,
'For we too are his offspring.'" (Acts 17:22-34)

Jesus used stories to relate the gospel to Israel because
that was the educational method of the day. However, Paul
was confronted with an audience that was philosophical in
nature. Because of that, Paul communicated the good news
from a philosophical perspective. In that way, Paul became
the philosopher for Christianity by making a philosophical
argument about the person of Christ. Paul's audience here
was not interested in stories about Jesus or a personal story
about how Jesus made him feel. They wanted to think and
debate, so Paul served up a philosophical line of reasoning
that he probably hoped would cause them to think further
with him on the relevance of Jesus. Paul had to catch their
attention and approach them where they were.

Paul made this argument using an altar dedicated to an
unknown god. Visually and verbally, Paul used the altar to
an unknown god to share the message of the incarnation of
Jesus. It was a stroke of genius. Paul recognized the
Athenians' interest in religion and used that interest to introduce them to the one God who sent Jesus into the world.

WHERE PEOPLE ARE

In the Acts passage quoted above, Paul sees something he
can use in order to begin where the people are and then
guide them to a new perspective. In verses 16-21, he starts
with the synagogue, moves to the marketplace, and then is
taken to the Areopagus to continue the debate. Every place
he went, Paul clearly articulated the message in ways that
people could understand. Obviously, it worked. He caught
the attention of the Epicureans and Stoics who wanted to

delve further into what he was saying. In order to make it happen, Paul went to them rather than waiting for an invitation.

The message of the gospel has to go where people are located. The call to follow Jesus did not mean the disciples would stay together enjoying one mountaintop experience after another. Jesus intended the church to be out in the world, and he sent his followers to where people lived their everyday lives.

> Then Jesus called the twelve together and gave them power and authority over all demons and to cure diseases, and he sent them out to proclaim the kingdom of God and to heal. He said to them, "Take nothing for your journey, no staff, nor bag, nor bread, nor money—not even an extra tunic. Whatever house you enter, stay there, and leave from there. Wherever they do not welcome you, as you are leaving that town shake the dust off your feet as a testimony against them." They departed and went through the villages, bringing the good news and curing diseases everywhere. (Luke 9:1-6)

People came to Jesus and his disciples for healing and teaching, but many more needed to hear the story of the closeness of the kingdom of God. Jesus knew the importance of going to people. Some people would not try to find Jesus, either because of their personality type, economic circumstances, or other personal situations that prevented them. The people who came were important, but so were those who did not come. Jesus sent the disciples out to do the work of God in the world. By doing so, the disciples were invited into the mission of God and were able to extend that mission outside the small area that Jesus himself covered.

As they went, the disciples were to rely on God and the hospitality of people. The mission would not bring the disciples great wealth; instead, it would bring them close to people. Living together and sharing the hospitality of human companionship created opportunities to talk with one another about important things, such as the story of God's relationship with people. The good news was shared not only in great and grandiose events, but also in one-on-one conversation in small-group settings. The sharing of the good news formed relationships and bonds; it built communities of faith who carried a common story. Those who did not want to listen were not forced into the relationship; rather, they were allowed to continue their way of life. However, those who wanted to listen to the message and were touched by it had their lives changed. Such relational evangelism is timeless and not bound by culture.

Our challenge is how to reach people intentionally where they are, just as Jesus and the disciples modeled for us. In the context of today, this type of evangelism is necessary and involves reaching out to people in both the physical and virtual worlds. People today are located in both worlds, and people today have the need for relationships.

The call to move out into the world echoes repeatedly in the Scriptures. Acts records two separate accounts of God directing the early church to reach out to people outside the Jewish community. The call was to go to all people wherever they were located, no matter who they were, and to announce the good news.[2] First is the account in Acts 10 of the Spirit of God urging Peter to come and share the story of Jesus with a devout centurion named Cornelius. While in prayer, Cornelius saw a vision of God's angel who told him to send for Peter. He sent two of his men, and as the men approached the city where Peter was, the text says that Peter was in prayer. He became hungry and fell into a trance while waiting for food. God gave him a vision that showed all kinds of animals, many of whom were forbidden for Jews to consume. "Get up, Peter; kill and eat," God said. When Peter protested, God added, "What God has made clean, you must not call profane" (vv. 13, 15). This happened three times, and Peter was puzzled about it. Then the men Cornelius sent arrived at the house where Peter was staying. The next day, Peter went with them to see Cornelius, who explained his vision and indicated that he was ready to hear what Peter had to say.

> Then Peter began to speak to them: "I truly understand that God shows no partiality, but in every nation anyone who fears him and does what is right is acceptable to him. You know the message he sent to the people of Israel, preaching peace by Jesus Christ—he is Lord of all. That message spread throughout Judea, beginning in Galilee after the baptism that John announced: how God anointed Jesus of Nazareth with the Holy Spirit and with power; how he went about doing good and healing all who were oppressed by the devil, for God was with him. We are witnesses to all that he did both in Judea and in Jerusalem. They put him to death by hanging him on a tree; but God raised him on the third day and allowed him to appear, not to all the people but to us who were chosen by God as witnesses, and who ate and drank with him after he rose from the dead. He commanded us to preach to the people and to testify that he is the one ordained by God as judge of the living and the dead. All the prophets testify about him that everyone who believes in him receives forgiveness of sins through his name."

While Peter was still speaking, the Holy Spirit fell upon all who heard the word. The circumcised believers who had come with Peter were astounded that the gift of the Holy Spirit had been poured out even on the Gentiles, for they heard them speaking in tongues and extolling God. Then Peter said, "Can anyone withhold the water for baptizing these people who have received the Holy Spirit just as we have?" So he ordered them to be baptized in the name of Jesus Christ. Then they invited him to stay for several days. (Acts 10:34-48)

Peter was called to go where the people searched for God. In responding, Peter committed a number of Jewish taboos. However, in Peter's vision God expanded the meaning of what is sacred. The message of the good news was intended for all people, regardless of their circumstances or life situation. The call was simply to go, and the response for Peter's willingness to extend the story to them was the coming of the Holy Spirit onto the entire household.

A similar event occurred in the life of Paul and is recorded in Acts 16. In this situation, a vision encourages Paul to come to Macedonia to share the good news.

They went through the region of Phrygia and Galatia, having been forbidden by the Holy Spirit to speak the word in Asia. When they had come opposite Mysia, they attempted to go into Bithynia, but the Spirit of Jesus did not allow them; so, passing by Mysia, they went down to Troas. During the night Paul had a vision: there stood a man of Macedonia pleading with him and saying, "Come over to Macedonia and help us." When he had seen the vision, we immediately tried to cross over to Macedonia, being convinced that God had called us to proclaim the good news to them. We set sail from Troas and took a straight course to Samothrace, the following day to Neapolis, and from there to Philippi, which is a leading city of the district of Macedonia and a Roman colony. We remained in this city for some days. On the sabbath day we went outside the gate by the river, where we supposed there was a place of prayer; and we sat down and spoke to the women who had gathered there. A certain woman named Lydia, a worshiper of God, was listening to us; she was from the city of Thyatira and a dealer in purple cloth. The Lord opened her heart to listen eagerly to what was said by Paul. When she and her household were baptized, she urged us, saying, "If you have judged me to be faithful to the Lord, come and stay at my home." And she prevailed upon us. (Acts 16:6-15)

There is consistency in both texts in the need for the church to go where people are in order to share the good news. The biblical record demonstrates what God can do when the church is willing to go outside the comfortable to the edges of ministry to meet people. A final example is the story of Philip in Acts, who is called by God to travel on a particular road. He meets an Ethiopian eunuch and interprets a Scripture passage from Isaiah for him, leading the eunuch to become a Christ follower and to ask for baptism (Acts 8:26-40).

God blesses such unselfish, courageous acts by moving the hearts of people. Philip did not hesitate; he responded to the need he saw and helped the Ethiopian understand the Scriptures and how it related to Jesus. Philip went and responded; he reached out to one who sought understanding, and God worked in the man's heart to bring him to the moment when he was ready to be baptized. Then Philip went off on another mission. Reaching out with the gospel does not stop, but continues to press forward to new places. To communicate the gospel, the early church had to be ready to move where the Holy Spirit directed them. The biblical mandate is go to all people wherever they are, and God will move in their hearts and lives to establish a relationship with them. In this scenario, it is less about us and more about God. God calls, God directs, God moves, and God changes the hearts of humanity.

Reaching out by going to the people is consistent with the traditions of the church. Every faith community has individuals and groups that reach out to people around them. Some people concentrate on reaching out to help with local needs, and others aid countries far away. Some faith communities have well-known examples of people reaching out with the gospel message, such as Stanley Livingston who dedicated his life to working with people in Africa or Father Damian who eventually sacrificed his life to bring hope to the leper community in Hawaii. Others are locally known and respected for their faith expressions of reaching out with the gospel message.

John Wesley, Anglican priest and founder of the Methodist movement, is another of the many examples of someone who took the love of God directly to the people. He did this in numerous ways. He felt as though the church of his day had forsaken the poor and oppressed. The Methodist movement began as a way of developing a deeper spirituality in the Anglican Church as people came together in small groups and took ministry to the streets of England, serving in jails and on the streets where people lived. When the Anglican Church refused to give Wesley a pulpit from which to preach, he preached in the fields and streets. It was something priests did not do in that day, and at first Wesley himself was against it. Eventually, however, Wesley realized that field preaching was an effective way of reaching into the lives of people. In his journal, Mr. Wesley wrote about his experiences with field preaching.

> Sun. 28.—I was invited by Mr. U., the Minister of Goodshaw, to preach in his church. I began reading Prayers at seven; but perceiving the church would scarce contain half of the congregation, after Prayers I went out, and standing on the church-yard wall, in a place shaded from the sun, explained and enforced those words in the Second Lesson, "Almost thou persuadest me to be a Christian."
>
> I wonder at those who still talk so loud of the indecency of field-preaching. The highest indecency is in St. Paul's church, when a considerable part of the congregation are asleep, or talking, or looking about, not minding a word the Preacher says. On the other hand, there is the highest decency in a churchyard or field, when the whole congregation behave and look as if they saw the Judge of all, and heard him speaking from heaven.
>
> At one I went to the Cross in Bolton. There was a vast number of people, but many of them utterly wild. As soon as I began speaking, they began thrusting to and fro; endeavouring to throw me down from the steps on which I stood. They did so once or twice; but I went up again, and continued my discourse. They then began to throw stones; at the same time some got upon the Cross behind me to push me down; on which I could not but observe, how God overrules even the minutest circumstances. One man was bawling just at my ear, when a stone struck him on the cheek, and he was still. A second was forcing his way down to me, till another stone hit him on the forehead: It bounded back, the blood ran down, and he came no farther. The third, being got close to me, stretched out his hand, and in the instant a sharp

stone came upon the joints of his fingers. He shook his hand, and was very quiet till I concluded my discourse and went away.[3]

Even amid great personal danger, John Wesley took the gospel message to the people. In his day, the Church of England no longer inspired people with the gospel. He described a church where there was disinterest in the act of worship itself. He left the formal pulpit behind and moved into the streets and fields. There he found receptive audiences who wanted to hear the gospel and even aided him by preventing people who tried to stop him. Wesley draws a sharp contrast between those who slept in the church and those in the fields who longed to hear. He was determined to preach the gospel message and live it out so that God's power could transform people. He was willing to do anything necessary to make that happen, even if it meant changing the way he shared the message.

INNOVATION

The history of the church shows a tradition of adapting to changing times. This is not acquiescing to societal pressures, but rather using the elements of society to help people experience the presence of a loving God. If we believe God created the entire universe and everything within it, then most anything has the potential of expressing the presence of God. The church needs to be in the world, pointing to the ways God reaches out to all people.

Modern society challenges the church to innovate and adopt the elements found in society to communicate the gospel of Christ. The gospel message must be relevant to the concerns and issues of the world and culture. If not, people will see it as extraneous to their lives and thus not be willing to explore the religious dimensions of human existence. Unconditional love, the kind of love demonstrated by God in the life, death and resurrection of Jesus, can have a huge impact particularly in the lives of people who face rejection by society at large. It is essential to tailor the gospel message to the language and imagery of people's lives.

If the church is to be faithful, then it must move with the Spirit of God. God's Spirit is not stagnant; rather, it moves in people's lives to create change and discipleship. God's Spirit moves us in unimaginable ways to mold us into the image of God found in Christ. To effect such change, God challenges our status quo. Jesus constantly challenged traditional ways of thinking. He was particularly hard on the religious leaders and those who felt they fully understood God. Jesus challenged the religious elite to see their sinfulness and come to a renewed relationship with God. Jesus reinterpreted the Scriptures with new understandings and went against social barriers and taboos. Jesus also challenged members of the religious establishment who had helped build those barriers and had become more interested in maintaining their positions of power than in serving God. Jesus was not as concerned about being religious as he was about following God. Jesus was an innovator who tried to help people see God in new ways.

Traditionally, the church is at its best when it innovates, not maintains. The church is at its best when it lives on the edge, trusting God's Spirit to move through it. The church becomes an exciting place when it leads people to experience God's presence in their daily lives. In order to be part of the lives of people, the church has to understand and use the familiar objects and images of the society and give them new meaning.

In the past, the church has been adept at using elements of society and adapting social images and language to the Christian message. When Christ followers sought to establish a festival to celebrate the birth of Jesus, one theory is that they chose to use a date from the Roman calendar that already had special meaning. December 25 was around the date of the festival of the sun god. The festival was associated with the equinox, which marked the time when the days begun to grow longer. Since it was celebrated as the birth of the sun god, the church adopted that day to proclaim the birth of the Son of God.

Church architecture was also adapted from the Roman temples and public buildings. After Emperor Constantine made Christianity the religion of the Roman Empire, the church came out of hiding and began to worship in public buildings. Until that time, the possibility of persecution was too intense to gather in large public areas for worship. With that threat gone, the church took the basilica as its worship building style. The original Roman basilica was a public hall designed to accommodate large numbers of people. People came to the basilica for various types of business. The basilicas held the stock exchanges, law courts, business offices, and administrative offices. Christians adapted the basilica for religious purposes. The basic shape of the basilica remained rectangular with two or more semicircular apses. However, the entrance was moved from the long side to the short side.[4] Architecturally, the basilica was a bridge between the old Roman Empire and the new Christian church.

> The spiritualizing of the secular Roman design is expressed not only in the realignment of the building's axis (so as to focus one's whole experience on the center) but in its extreme simplicity of structure and the lightness

of its bearing walls and columns. Roman mass—huge walls and ponderous weight, sculptured surfaces in relief and recess, and whole populations of statuary—has been lightened, rarefied, smoothed; we could say it has been "dematerialized" to suit the new orientation toward the spiritual rather than the physical world.[5]

The invention of the printing press forever changed the world. Through the printing press, for the first time words and images were readily available to everyone. Before this invention, individuals copied books by hand, which made them too expensive for many people to afford. Usually only the wealthy owned books. Because books were not widely accessible, reading was not considered important. During that time, the church used images and icons to teach religious stories to illiterate people. The printing press made books more affordable and created a reason for people to learn to read. It helped introduce new ideas and concepts and created an opportunity for people to educate themselves.

The Reformation spread in large part due to the printing press. Before the beginnings of this movement, the printing press had already begun to disperse reading material and religious works.[6] This new forum for exploring ideas prepared people's minds to read and digest information via books. No longer was reading only for the learned or religious professionals. Now more and more people could read and decide for themselves what they thought about world events and new religious, scientific, and social concepts. The world was beginning to open up.

The printing press quickly became a tool for the reformers to publish their writings widely across Europe to a growing reading public.

The printing-press was important in the early spread of the Reformation. The writings of the first German reformers (Luther and Melanchthon) reached a comparatively wide public in printed form within weeks, and were soon read in Paris and Rome. At the height of the Reformation, in the last years of Luther's life, busy printers enabled the anonymous work *Beneficio di Christo* (which more than any other book spread the doctrine of justification by faith in Italy) to sell 40,000 copies in Venice alone after its publication there in 1543.[7]

The power of this new technology was quickly adapted to spread the Reformation's message and global changing perspectives to all people. The Reformers saw the power in this new technology and changed how they communicated new ideas and concepts. The printing press was able to move the writings of the reformers off the church walls and doors and into people's homes. This gave people time to reflect on the meaning of the words and talk together about the new ideas. No longer would the church or intellectuals hold captive new and challenging concepts and ideas. With knowledge came power. The reformers did not shy away from using the newest technology of their day to publicize their challenges to the church. Those who heard them, being tired of the church's abuses over the years, responded in positive ways. People were empowered through the transmission of knowledge to respond to the issues surrounding the Reformation.

There were other innovations by people who wanted to share the good news with those who had become jaded about the church. Christians have adapted popular music, forms of art, and other elements of culture to express the good news in ways people can understand. Connecting the real lives of people with the gospel makes the gospel relevant to their lives. When the gospel is relevant and understandable, God can use the message to influence lives.

In order to help people respond to the new movement of God's Spirit in the world, John Wesley created a small-group ministry to support and guide people in living out the good news in their daily lives. Wesley believed that people expressed their faith in daily living and working, and he tried to provide the resources necessary to help them. Wesley's innovative small groups provided a place where people could gather for learning and support. They studied the Scriptures, prayed together, talked together about the challenges of living out the good news of Jesus in their lives, and supported one another in their struggles. The classes, bands, and societies created a new lay movement in the church that energized the Christian faith. It was successful in large part because it was relevant to the struggles and challenges of living the Christian life in the world. People were touched with the message because it met them where they lived.

NOTES

1. "The Electronic Ben Franklin: The Quotable Franklin," http://www.ushistory.org/franklin/quotable/singlehtml.htm (accessed 20 August 2008).

2. It should be noted that there was great debate about whether to include Gentiles in the Christian community. The early church was divided over who was acceptable for membership and whether members had to first renounce their Gentile lifestyle and become a Jew, including circumcision for the men. The Jerusalem Council decided that Gentiles should be included in the life of the church without circumcision, but it certainly was not an easy decision for Peter to reach out to people he thought were outside of God's interest.

3. *The Works of John Wesley*, vol. 2, CD-ROM (Franklin TN: Providence House Publishers, 1995) 113.

4. *Art Through the Ages*, 6th ed., rev. by Horst de la Croix and Richard G. Tansey (New York: Harcourt Brace Jovanovich, Inc., 1975) 220.

5. Ibid., 251.

6. Tim Dowley, John Briggs, David Wright, and Robert Linder, eds., *Eerdman's Handbook to the History of Christianity* (Grand Rapids: Wm. B. Eerdmans, 1977) 352.

7. Ibid., 352.

TOOLS FOR COMMUNICATING: WHERE CAN THE CHURCH GO?

Where does the church go from here? If I listed the specific technologies and methods the church could currently employ in the service of the gospel, in a few months it would be out of date. Technology and communication tools change rapidly. Churches need to begin exploring the use of technology by deciding *why* they wish to use it. Each congregation has a unique answer to this question. Do we want to use technology because everyone else is using it? Do we perceive that growing churches benefit from the use of technology? A more meaningful way of looking at technology use in the church is to ask whether technology will help the church better communicate the gospel and invite people into a meaningful relationship with God. Part of that discussion includes what type of technology is needed, such as technology in worship or education, social networking, or advancements for the church office.

Computers and technology are an integral part of human life. CPUs and laptops appear in many homes and workplaces in the United States. According to U.S. Census Bureau statistics, computer use has increased dramatically since 1984, when only 8.2 percent of households had a computer and no homes had Internet access. By 2003, 61.8 percent of U.S. homes, or 70 million households, had computers, and 62 million households, or 54.7 percent, accessed the Internet.[1]

The great increase of computers represents a dramatic change in the lifestyles of people in the United States and around the world. Computers connect people globally, offering the potential of sharing video, pictures, and emails with friends and relatives across the country and around the world. Computers allow faster and easier ways to communicate. Given the trend, it is certain that computer use will continue to increase in the coming years. Computers and advancing technology are clearly a part of human existence in real and dynamic ways. With new advances and the creation of ever-faster machines, the current generation that is growing up with computers will move into adulthood and change the ways the world functions. They will continue to expand use of the Internet for research, entertainment, social networking, and a variety of other activities; it is simply a part of their ordinary lifestyle.

Even with such dramatic technology changes, the church should not use technology simply for the sake of using technology. It is easy to become attracted to using "cool," glitzy electronic gadgets merely because they are available. Not every piece of technology is functional in and beneficial to every congregation, however. Some types of technology may even be counter-productive for a particular congregation. Church members are wise to spend time considering why they want to use technology and what will work best in their particular facility and for their unique ministry in the community.

How does a particular tool fit into my church? Is it something so complicated that neither the church nor visitors will respond to it? Is it something that will gather dust in a few months because no one knows how or wants to use it? If the church is considering using a new tool, someone must know how it works, and the church must have a vision for how it will help communicate the gospel.

General guides can help church members discern how to approach the proclamation of the gospel. Answering questions like these can direct a church to the proper technology for its specific needs: To which familiar elements of society do people relate every day? What are people's needs both in our church and in the surrounding community? What available technology can be innovated or used as is to communicate the gospel in an understandable way? Each congregation is unique and has an exclusive set of positive and negative elements. Additionally, each generation and cultural setting may have different answers. By taking time to consider these questions, a church can discover what technology and techniques might enhance its ministry.

FINE ARTS

Someone once said a "picture is worth a thousand words." If this is true, then the fine arts are a valuable tool for Christian communication. Throughout human history, artists have depicted scenes from the Bible and concepts of theology, touching people's souls with a new sense of spirituality. They used familiar images that people understood. It is interesting to note that images of Jesus are found in many different nations, and that each artist uses the physical characteristics of his or her society to depict him. African art often depicts Jesus as African, Asian art as Asian, and so on. Such artwork helps to bring Jesus into the lives of people by using images to which they can relate the most. It is helpful to see Jesus as a part of our lives, and it brings Jesus closer to us and how we live.

Negatively, art that depicts God with "our" human characteristics also points to the fact that we tend to make God in our image rather than seeing ourselves in the image of God. Such mistaken efforts can generate human pride and arrogance as we begin to think we are somehow more like God than other peoples of the earth. It is a double-edged sword. Art can bring new understanding of the divine, but it can also show our human arrogance in believing we can remake God into our image. The faith community can help us discern what concepts are mistaken.

Music is also used to communicate the gospel message to people of many cultures. Whether through drums, flutes, organs, stringed instruments, or other types, music communicates something beyond itself. Music is not static, but changes through the ages, and the music of the church changes with it. The instruments the churches use have included piano, organ, bells, and keyboards. Different churches use different instruments, and each provides meaning in the act of worship. Some people embrace the change and others fight it, but if the church focuses on reaching and teaching people the grace of God, its people will be flexible and open to such changes. Throughout history, when the church becomes rigid, it loses touch with people and risks being segregated from those who need the church community the most.

The church has used a great variety of ways to announce the story of the gospel. Each age, Christians have searched to discover the best ways to help people hear and respond. It is an ever-changing communication effort. We cannot be content to stop where we are in the belief that what worked twenty years ago will work in the present. The story of God's loving incarnation into human history is consistent; the means of telling the story constantly evolves to keep pace with the advancements of technology.

INNOVATION

Using technology requires innovation. The church has experience with adapting to changing times. As the way a culture communicates changes, the church must adapt to the changes to keep the message of the gospel relevant to society. The church cannot change for the sake of change alone; rather, the church innovates to communicate the good news more efficiently and clearly. Church people in every generation must explore the surrounding culture with the mindset of what they can adapt in order to communicate the good news. What aspects of the current cultural mind can the church use to create a positive message about the Reign of God? What can the church adapt from society in order to reach out to people in positive ways? The church took elements of Roman society to create the celebration of Christmas, adapted Roman architecture to build the first church buildings, and took advantage of the printing press to spread the good news. The modern church has the same calling and the same Spirit to follow into new ways of relating the gospel to people.

If we believe God is a creative God who has given us everything we have, then nearly anything can be used for the purposes of God. The challenge for the church is to explore ways of creatively using these new tools to announce the presence of God. It is by no means easy; communicating well takes work and study. What can we use to proclaim the gospel in ways to which people relate?

Every society has elements the church can use to communicate the gospel. Often such elements are overlooked or not considered because the gospel has never been communicated using that particular tool. I encourage you to view the sharing of the gospel as a dynamic exploration of new possibilities for proclaiming the ongoing presence and power of God.

FAMILIAR ELEMENTS

The church needs to relate to the world in its present state in order to be a transformative power in the community. The church cannot nostalgically force society to return to times gone by, but the church can adapt the message of the gospel to make it understandable to modern society. In this technological age, the church can quickly turn into a dinosaur. As we saw in the previous chapter, through the ages the church has used familiar elements in society to communicate the gospel message.

In our fast-paced technological world, it is easy to want to stick with the familiar ways of operating as the church. However, these ways are quickly, if not already, becoming alien to people who are not involved in the church. For example, in worship the church uses terms such as "hymn," "washed in the blood of the Lamb," "Gloria Patri," and others that are alien to unchurched people. Regular attenders know when to sit and stand, what to say when, and what happens during Eucharist or baptism. For people who have not been involved in the life of a congregation, adjusting to these habits is often a difficult transition. What can the church do to promote familiar terminology that helps people understand worship?

In Sunday school, leaders sometimes make assumptions about what people know. Sometimes they say something like, "You all know the familiar story about Noah." This may not be true, and even if everyone knows the story, people may not remember particular elements. The church must understand that people, particularly guests, may not have read the Bible or experienced worship enough to be familiar with various aspects of each. The church has to adapt some of the practices and take time to educate the congregation so people can make sense of tradition or of new changes.

The church has to struggle with the ideas, language, and practices of the culture. As we studied above, Jesus used culturally relevant images in parables and examples to teach about the Reign of God, and people responded to the power of his teaching. The church can recapture that powerful method by exploring how to make the message correspond to the real lives of people. The church today is called to study the experiences and technologies with which people are familiar and consider how to use them to communicate the gospel.

Cell phones, computers, movies, the Internet, podcasting, and community/social networking sites such as Facebook, YouTube, or Twitter are only a few of the examples of familiar elements of modern culture. Many people are comfortable with these elements of technology, and the church needs to stay current with them as well. Is the church podcasting sermons or other audio files? Is the church using social networking sites and airing videos that communicate the gospel in entertaining and meaningful ways? Is the church trying to be an important part of the online community, or is the church fighting against it in the vain hope of returning to the past? This is not the end of technological advances. The challenge for the church is to stay updated on popular technology and explore how to use it to attract people and communicate the gospel.

To effectively use technology and the familiar elements of everyday life, one must be open to teachable moments when people begin to seek answers to difficult issues. Occasions frequently arise when we can share something about the presence of God. It can happen online, in person, or during a brief encounter. While we are rarely fully prepared for teachable moments, our reactions to them can have long-lasting effects. As we have seen, Jesus used teachable moments throughout his ministry. For the church to be effective, Christians must be familiar with Scripture, cultural images, and modern language and understand differences in ages and each generation's perception of themselves, the world, and technology.

First, the church must help people inside and outside the church become more familiar with Scripture texts. This does not mean simply quoting verses or reciting surface understandings of Scripture. Rather, it means a willingness to dig deeply into the text, looking at the Scriptures critically and wrestling with their meanings in antiquity and for the world today. In this technological world, it seems that people either dismiss Scripture or accept it without exploring the variety of meanings a particular text may have. In many churches, it is apparent that the Sunday school is quickly becoming a lost time for the Christian community to explore the Bible and theology. People send their children for moral training, but many adults seem uninterested in Bible study. To reach out to this world of critical thinkers, with a variety of cultures and religious traditions, the church must teach its own traditions and understandings to people. Certainly, people in the church will not have all the answers, but rather they should demonstrate a willingness to wrestle critically with Scripture and theology. In this age, people will not always listen if the story is too simplistic. If we can't find ways to apply the gospel to the familiar elements of human life, then the gospel will not speak to people.

The gospel story is in some ways like an onion. An onion has many layers, and peeling back one layer reveals yet another one. It is easy to find new meanings in a Scripture passage each time one reads it. Also, in reading Scripture and trying to understand its depth, one will think of new ways to communicate the story. We can make the Scriptures alive by living into the stories so that they become our stories, not just stories in an ancient book. The church brings the Scripture to life, and it is through God's grace and Spirit that the story enlivens the ministry of the church as it presents the gospel in new ways.

To accomplish this, the church must explore the society around it. What languages are people using? What images and stories do they use to express meaning? What does the church have to say to the problems and issues of society, and how can it communicate in understandable ways? The church has to look beyond the doors and walls to the society around it. How can the gospel story touch the lives of people outside the church? What do people look like and sound like? Are they different from those "inside the church" racially, economically, or culturally? If so, why has the church not invited them into the church community? Is technology, language, or social understanding a barrier? If so, how can the church overcome the barriers?

In this technological age, those with means and those without means are growing further and further apart. Technology can be a dividing wall that keeps out those who cannot afford it. How can school-aged children without computers and access to technology learn at the same rate as children who have technology readily available? Can they have the same opportunities and develop the same skills and social interactions as their peers? How can the church respond to such social and economic injustice? Communicating the gospel in the technological age is not only about using technology in worship or Sunday school. It also means responding to the issues technology raises in ways that help bring justice and equality to all God's children. To communicate the gospel message to our technological age is not just an invitation to a meaningful relationship with God, but a way for the church to reach out in the love of Christ to change people's lives by challenging the social, economic, and technological forces that divide humanity. Sharing the gospel is helping people develop a sense of self-worth, regardless of their daily access to the latest advances.

Communicating the gospel in the technological age also means understanding how people of various generations use technology. Technological use in the United States is not yet to a point where the church can stop sending paper newsletters or other hard-copy items through the mail. Many people are not computer literate, and the church cannot ignore people who do not have computers. Not everyone is ready to shift to an all-digital world; some people simply love to sit and read a paper book. Others prefer the computer screen. The technological world as it exists today calls for the church to respond to people and society in a variety of ways, not just digitally. On the other hand, not using advanced technology may alienate younger generations. It is a balancing act that each church must attempt. Who are the members of our church? What generations are represented? How do they use technology? What kinds of technology are they using currently, and how can the church use it to communicate the gospel to them?

The answers to such questions can help your church to begin to find familiar elements from culture to use in communicating the gospel. It requires an honest look at the church, at society, and at people around the church community who are not involved in the life of the church. Such an honest assessment can be troubling and difficult. Sometimes the church does not want to see the answers or does not have the courage to leave behind familiar ways of doing things to explore new ways of proclaiming the old gospel message. If the church can find the courage to explore the edges of sharing the gospel using familiar elements in human society, God will bless the efforts. The blessing can come in many ways: more members, spiritual growth in the church, more fulfilling service, better understanding of the Bible, Christian theology, or the issues of society. Success is not always seen as growth in numbers; it is more about growth toward God and neighbors.

WHERE PEOPLE ARE

The church is called to go where people are. That is the way to get to know people and build a relationship that draws people to God. Jesus and his disciples did not set up camp somewhere and wait for people to come to them. Rather, Jesus and his disciples went where people lived and worked to share with them the story of the gospel message. They traveled, ate in people's homes, and responded to requests to come and help with specific situations. They had no building or official residence as their headquarters. They went where people were.

The church has followed that pattern. John Wesley went outside the church to the poor and disenfranchised; George Whitefield used field preaching to share the good news with those outside the church, missionaries went to live and work in different cultures around the world, and the church continued the tradition set by Jesus to go where people were. As we consider the present technologically growing world, the church has to ask itself where people are located today. Can meaningful outreach occur without the church reaching out to people where they are?

Where are people today? The simplistic answer is "everywhere." We need to look at the multiple worlds in which people function. First is the physical world that we see, hear, and experience with our human range of sensory mechanisms. Then there is the virtual world of the digital, a different world from the physical and yet nonetheless real. Thinking about both worlds in terms of the ways people function and form relationships is important for the church. Without such dialogue, how can the church discover the areas where it might reach out to people? People live in both worlds, the physical and virtual, and to reach out fully, the church must have a vital presence in both worlds.

The Physical World

This physical world has been humanity's home since the creation of human beings. In the physical world people, can be found at home, at work, away on vacation, and at other gathering places. Even in our technological world, people are still on the move and doing all sorts of activities. One of the visions portrayed about technology is that it has tied people to computers and kept them away from one another. As the world becomes wireless, technology can go where we go. In some ways, the virtual world goes with us into the physical world. The ties of communication are never far away, even if we are far away from home.

As in the past, the church is called today to go out into the world where people are. It is a call to go to the soccer fields, shopping malls, coffee shops, and other places where people gather. It is not a call to be obnoxious about being there. The church community does not necessarily have to cart a busload of people to a business or shopping mall with the intention of converting or talking with every person they see. Instead, as people move in and out of their normal connections, they do so as a part of the Christian community. Communicating the gospel does not have to take place in prearranged times, but can occur as people interact with one another. It is more a matter of being ready to respond when the subject arises; ready for teachable moments that arise as human beings relate and talk with one another; ready to share with people what God has already shared with us. It is not preaching or forcing the gospel on people as much as it is relating something that is important to us. The other side to this relational evangelism is our willingness to listen to what people say to us about their beliefs and life situations. There are many types of stressors in this fast-paced technological world, and people often need relief. As followers of Christ, we can provide relief for people by listening and understanding, and then by sharing hope in God though Christ.

We seem to have lost this aspect of Christianity. The church creates programs, squeezing time out of busy family lives in order to draw many people to events. When some do not attend, people tend to view their absence as a strike against the church community. People easily jump to the conclusion that something must be wrong because someone was not present. Part of the reality of the physical world is that it is a busy place where people choose among family events, work obligations, and household chores, and the church quickly becomes one more thing that vies for priority.

As the church envisions communicating with the physical world, perhaps we should focus less emphasis on programs and more emphasis on education and helping people be Christian witnesses wherever they find themselves. It may require re-visioning what people think of church and why they come to church. The church is not a social organization or a place that will meet all of one's needs and wants. The church is not a full-service convenience stop. Rather, the purpose of the church is to make disciples of Jesus Christ. That purpose means the church is a training ground to help people communicate the gospel message in what they say and how they live. The church then becomes a community striving to learn all they can, be all they can, and reach out all they can, all for the glory of God.

One of the vital ways of helping the church become a disciple-making community and training ground is to create small groups where people can share together the gospel message. Small groups provide a community of people who can share their struggles and discuss how they are trying to be witnesses in the world. This is less a program people attend and more an opportunity for people to learn about and participate in the work of the gospel in the world.

Rather than a place where people come to watch a good performance, the church becomes a place where people are made into disciples.

For the church to be effective in the physical world, it must reach out through its members and help them grow continually in discipleship. If people are not growing, they are stagnating in the faith or coming to church to be entertained. It is easy to think that coming on Sunday is the sum of the Christian obligation to God. We came to church on Sunday, so we are good until next week. Or there are the C and E people, who come to church only on Christmas and Easter as their fulfillment of a twice yearly obligation to God. Vital churches help people learn to live out a life of faith wherever they are. Without people willing to live out a Christian lifestyle, the gospel may never reach beyond the walls of the church building.

In this technological world, people's time is stretched and strained. Yet Christians can be the church wherever they are. One does not have to attend meetings at the church to be a Christian witness in business and other relationships. Through worship and education, the church can prepare people to be Christian witnesses. However, the church sometimes over-programs in the name of discipleship and loses touch with its purpose, which is to nurture a meaningful relationship with Jesus Christ that takes people out into the world to share the gospel.

The church is called to be a living disciple of Jesus. This does not mean the church must offer numerous involved programs in order to be a faithful witness. Nor is there an excuse for doing nothing under the guise that the congregation comes together on Sunday and lives faithfully the rest of the week. Rather, the church community is called to help people know God and acknowledge that God's presence is with them wherever they are. The church is called to be a healing hospital so that the message of the good news is spread. The church is not a place for saints to gather, but a place where people come and find grace for their lives in the midst of hardships. The church is a place for the broken and ostracized, for all God's children to come and learn what it means to be a disciple.

In the physical world, the church is a place to find grace in order to live grace. A longtime Christian man told me a story. I suspect it could be repeated in many places across the world. Every Sunday when he left for church, his neighbor stood outside washing his car. The two exchanged hellos, and each one then went his separate way. This continued for some twenty years, week after week. Then one Sunday as the man left for church, he found his neighbor standing in his driveway and wearing a suit and tie. His neighbor said, "I don't know where you go every Sunday, but you have what I need."

A living faith in this world can have an influential impact on people. Had the man asked his neighbor to come to church earlier, the neighbor might have turned him down and their dialogue might have become strained. By being a living witness through the way he conducted his life, God used the man to touch the heart of his neighbor who began a search for the source of this man's abundant life. The most vital witness of the church in the physical world occurs outside the walls of the church in the everyday lives of Christian people. It can be as simple as offering a warm smile and a word of grace and encouragement to someone having a bad day, or witnessing to the presence of the gospel when we work with Habitat for Humanity, serve on mission projects, and help people in the church connect their faith with the realities of life.

THE VIRTUAL WORLD

With the advent of the Internet, our world changed. A new world was slowly created through computers. This new digital world is not like that found in the movie *The Matrix*, with people hooked to machines who only dream a real life, but this virtual world is another reality, and human beings exist within this world in important ways. It must also be stated that, like any part of creation, this virtual world is used for good or evil. The tool itself is amoral; the people behind this virtual world decide the level of morality of the different websites. Some people in this virtual world seek the presence of God. The church is called to be present wherever people seek God, serving as a witness for the living God and the hope God offers. People are online daily for work, school, email, investments, or other reasons. The Internet is a world where the church can be a real presence in people's lives.

The virtual world is a dynamic place. At first, only scientists accessed this world, and then dial-up into the virtual world was offered, even though it was slow and cumbersome. Next came high-speed connections, wireless access in buildings, and wireless access outside and on cell phones. Who knows what might come next? The virtual world has become so much a part of our lives that on this digital platform, bills are paid, banking transactions completed, entertainment sought out, emails exchanged, and activities interrupted at the sounds of incoming texts, instant messages, and the next tweet.

People are online looking for meaning and belonging. One can argue that this may be not the best place to search for it, but no one can deny that people use the Internet for this reason. Communities are formed that offer help to people with various issues and problems, and discussion boards develop with people sharing intimate details of their lives. Sites like My Space, YouTube, Twitter, or Facebook give people the opportunity to express themselves through music, videos, photos, or words. People begin blogs to share information and to discuss issues of the day. The amount of information that can be gathered off community sites is almost overwhelming. Without a doubt, the church needs to be there.

The church can reach people in the virtual world. We are called to be where people are in the virtual world just as surely as we are called to be where people are in the physical world. The church must ask where people are found online and create a presence there to reach out to them. Words, images, and other media should be carefully selected to communicate the gospel message effectively. Understanding the potential requires time, research, and the help of those who are on social networking sites. Involving children and youth in this mission of the church is a wonderful way to help them learn something about sharing the gospel message in an online presence.

People often say children and youth are the future of the church. While that may be true, it cannot be overlooked that they are also the church *now*. The only way they will fully understand what it means to be the church is by living out faith in the physical and virtual world. The church is called to make disciples of all people regardless of age, gender, or other human-devised barriers. To reach out into the worlds of life, the church is called to listen to those who are a part of each generation. Only by listening and valuing people can the church make a difference in their lives and also communicate the gospel.

Communication in the virtual world is different. It is audio and visual; it is an image-based world where people express themselves creatively. For the church to be a real presence in the virtual world, it has to create sites that reflect the language and culture online while maintaining the gospel message. To be effective, the church's message must be seen and heard, active and attractive; the gospel has to catch people's attention and communicate something about the love and graciousness of God in a way that invites people into community with God and humanity. The following sections explore various aspects of the virtual world.

YouTube

People enjoy the creativity of social networking sites. On sites such as YouTube, people create and upload videos in order to share with the world something about who they are and what they believe. The church can do the same thing by uploading creative videos with a gospel message. On YouTube, churches and individuals upload lectures, music videos, and other media to communicate with the world, and any faith community can upload their own efforts to reach out.

Churches must ensure that anything they post online is well done. Whether one posts a theological perspective, an interesting story set to video, or a music video produced by the church, YouTube offers a unique opportunity for self-expression and communication of faith. People of all ages are producing videos on YouTube, and the church can combine the efforts of adults, youth, and children so that it not only connects with the youth of today, but also has the support of the history and tradition of the church. Such cooperative efforts make the message stronger in content, and still allow youth to have the creative power to make it real to other youth. By posting on sites like YouTube, the church becomes accessible to anyone who is a part of that community. That means your church, youth group, or other group in the church can have their videos viewed by people who may not necessarily go to a church website.

Facebook

Facebook offers people an opportunity to connect with friends and family and share about their lives. It is a way to find long-lost friends and interact with loved ones. One can share photos and stories and play games in the virtual world. Members express thoughts about current events in the world as well as their individual lives, sharing information quickly and easily. One can create groups and fan pages for those who share certain interests.

How can we discover God, or how can God discover us on Facebook? While God has no Facebook page or group, many who use the service claim to represent God. Can we find grace and the presence of God virtually? While God does not need the church or humanity to accomplish God's purposes, God uses both to spread the gospel message. Sharing the gospel face to face is essential, but there are other ways to spread God's love. The church has shared the gospel through the written word for centuries. Now, in the twenty-first century, we have access to a wide variety of new tools with which to share the written word, including the use of images and video. God uses such methods to reach people each day. When used with intentionality, Facebook allows the Christian community to create pages and groups that serve as important ways of telling people about the presence of God.

Facebook offers many interesting possibilities for the church to reach out to members as well as nonmembers.

Facebook provides people and groups that are part of the church an easy way to stay in contact with one another on a daily basis. A Christian education group or small group can post announcements about upcoming events or reminders about planned activities. People can share prayer concerns throughout the week, and the group can decide whether to make the pages public or private. It can also be fun to share pictures of activities, fun stories about what happened during a particular activity, or joys/concerns. Facebook is also a way to communicate more serious thoughts, such as links to daily devotionals, Scripture verses, or inspirational points. Congregations can use Facebook to post events in the community of faith and as a way to reach out to congregants and others.

When groups go on mission trips, Facebook is a place to post pictures and information that people can easily access. Many places have Internet access, making it simple for mission groups to upload pictures, share stories, and even blog[2] about what happens on a trip. People at home can witness the trip as it occurs and stay updated on the group's progress.

Facebook offers an opportunity to be creative in reaching out to people who may not be part of the church. A congregation can set up a Facebook page or group that is open for anyone to join or view the content. Such an effort allows the church to have a presence at the heart of community websites. By leaving the site open to allow anyone to view it, creating a site that is attractive to the youth culture, and posting content that communicates to that generation and that invites without condemning, the church has great potential to reach many people.

Can the church or an individual create a Facebook site that presents the gospel in a way that interests people who are not in the church? It depends on how information is shared, including the use of language. Dozens of groups and individuals vie for people's attention. If the church is serious about reaching people with a fresh gospel message, it will intentionally seek creative ways of presenting the message to people who are not part of a church community. What kind of church Facebook page would invite people to return to it regularly?

Twitter

Twitter is a live tool with no delay in the delivery of one's thoughts. "Tweets" can be sent immediately to the computers or cell phones of anyone with a Twitter account, and even those without Twitter can access individual pages with a proper web address. Surely God can use such a powerful tool that reaches instantly around the world.

The advent and rapid spread of Twitter have opened new possibilities for the church to share the gospel in 140 characters or less. Twitter is a marvelous tool for Christians to express their faith around the world. It offers an opportunity to share Scripture, whether the particular verse speaks to a current world event or reflects an individual's personal journey. One can express theological thoughts, and others can tweet back immediately and add to the discussion. The possibility of a thought or comment reaching literally thousands of people is not out of the realm of possibility. Miracles are about timing, and God can certainly use a tweet to touch someone's life with the gospel.

One could use Twitter to market church events. Also, by tweeting a small amount of information and a link, one can generate traffic to a personal or church website. The potential for the spread of information is astounding, as one person might forward it to another, and so on. We never know whom God may send to the church or how God might use a tweet to touch someone's life in a positive way.

On Twitter the community of faith can keep in touch with groups who are on mission trips. Using tags in the tweets can help filter individual tweets from groups so that people who are interested can keep up with trips as events unfold. Imagine being at home or work and getting up-to-the-minute tweets from groups in your congregation who are involved in mission work in the community or elsewhere in the world. What a fantastic way to share what God is doing at that moment in their lives and the lives of those they serve!

Missionaries can use Twitter to talk about their ministries. Twitter provides a tool for missionaries to communicate in real time with congregations and people who support them in their work. They can share prayer concerns, exciting news, and specific needs and receive instant feedback. Truly, the possibilities are limitless in how Twitter could aid communication among people who are working for God.

Church Websites

By creating an Internet webpage, churches can share the gospel in many ways. Church websites often list events, provide downloadable bulletins and sermon podcasts, and share opportunities for service in the church. This is helpful for those who are part of the church and only use the site to get information. But what about those around the world who may not know about Christianity? What does your website offer visitors that will announce the good news of the gospel to them? What content does your website offer that will make people wonder about Christianity enough to begin seeking God in their lives? On the Internet, where the entire world has access to your page, do you only offer bulletins and newsletters, or do you invite them to know who Jesus is and experience the love of God shown in the incarnation? What does your church do online that it cannot do using paper bulletins and newsletters?

The church's website must be maintained. Church sites are notorious for providing outdated information. Someone must be in charge of ensuring that events, links, and dates are current. Why would anyone want to attend a church if the only available information is out of date?

The web has become the front door to the church for many people. Some say they would not attend a church that has no website. When people come to your website, what greets them? Is it cold and colorless, with no images but lots of links up and down the page? Or is it friendly and relational, inviting visitors to find out more? Technically able, relational, and artistic people should create the church's website. It must communicate more than information about the next Wednesday supper; it must communicate something about the church community and God.

The church can also support spiritual development via a website. How does your website touch people's spiritual lives? How does it bring people closer to God? A congregation can post daily devotions on a website. There are several ways of doing this. One is to find a site that posts strong devotional material and link to it from your church site. This is a simple way that requires little work from people in the church.

A more creative approach is to have people in the church write the material for the devotional site. There are many benefits to this approach. First, you publish an original devotional word for public access. Second and perhaps most important, people in the church grow in their spiritual journeys, as they are required to reflect upon their own walks with God. If the church guides individuals and encourages their gifts, they will grow in their understanding of themselves and of God. Another benefit is that if people know those who write the articles, they will be more likely to read them and share the site with others. This will bring more traffic to the site and increase the number of people the church reaches with the good news.

Many churches post sermons online. Perhaps the simplest way is to post text that people can read. The most dynamic way is to use websites that allow posting of video of the sermon and have it play back on computers or iPods with video capability. Sometimes this service is too costly, or it requires a password that not everyone may have. Still, it is a dynamic way to provide access to sermons preached at a church. No matter how the sermon is posted online, it may minister more to those who are already Christians rather than reaching someone who seeks God. However, we never know how God's Spirit will lead someone. The call of the church is to be open to as many possibilities as possible and leave responses to the movement of God's Spirit.

In addition to sermons, churches can offer music or other audio podcasts. Some issues exist concerning the broadcast of copyright materials, particularly with music, so the church needs to be aware of the various laws. But churches can podcast sermons, faith journey stories, or other stories that may be spiritually uplifting and are not copyrighted material. For instance, a church can provide a Scripture reading on an audio file along with a reflection by the pastor or another person that helps bring understanding to the text. A website visitor can download the podcast, upload it to an iPod or other media player, and listen as they walk, drive, or exercise. The church can provide a variety of materials or even suggest other places where people can download devotional materials for the iPod. The church does not have to produce it, but may simply look for what is available and tell people where to find it.

The church can post daily Scripture readings online in either audio or text form. Sometimes people want to start their day with Scripture, and it is easy to find online. The church can also offer verses as devotional material. Also, people who are visually handicapped may enjoy having access to an audio version. News about such a ministry could quickly spread through the community, and many people would find their way to the site. Then the church could explore other ways to help the visually impaired or others with physical challenges who can access the Internet.

Blogs

Churches can use blogs to reach out to people who enjoy sharing their thoughts and ideas with others. Blogs provide an opportunity to make faith statements about God and then invite responses from others in a non-threatening way. To do it well, the church can use an online blogging site or find a way of driving traffic to the church's website and then linking to the blog or creating one of its own. Without some means of communicating the blog's presence, it will never serve its full creative potential. Having a blog may challenge the church in some ways, as some of the comments may be unpleasant to read, but the church is not called to be available only in pleasant places. Grace and understanding are required when addressing messages that are hostile to the church's views. On the other hand, blogs and comments serve as an opportunity to communicate with those who are disenfranchised with the church and perhaps help them to reconsider their perception.

A negative response to the gospel is not a new problem. When Jesus preached, some people became angry about what he said and sometimes argued with him. When Peter preached, people were angry enough to arrest him; even at the celebration of Pentecost, Peter was questioned about the events. Some thought those who proclaimed the gospel at Pentecost were drunk and confused! When Paul preached, he was arrested, beaten, and jailed. These people from the Christian past proclaimed the gospel out in the world, not in the safety of the Christian community. Blogging offers an opportunity once again to take the good news of God's presence into the world to people who may have never heard the message. It gives the church a chance to hear about the broken reality of people's lives and reach them in a tangible way.

Text Messaging
Young people spend more time texting on cell phones than they do talking on them. Using one or more cell phone numbers, one can send a brief text message via computer or cell phone. If your church's outreach includes youth, texting can be a vital part of your ministry. A ministry leader could send reminders of events, a daily Scripture reading, prayers or prayer requests, poignant quotes, or messages to those going through difficulty. Text messages remind people that a caring community loves and supports them and thinks of them each day. Also, if someone has not been attending regularly, a text message invitation that the person is wanted and welcomed may help reconnect him or her with the church.

While it is essential to communicate with those outside the church, people who are a part of a church also need to know they are missed when they don't attend. It is important to find a balance that communicates love and concern without condemnation. Sending brief text messages, perhaps with Scripture references from a missed Bible study and an upbeat note, can let people know they are missed and encourage them to return when possible. The church is called to make disciples, and to fulfill that call, the church must strive to reach out to all God's people.

Visual Media

Many of us receive stories from movies, television, and other forms of media, whereas our ancestors and other parts of the world hear stories told by storytellers. The church can use media in order to connect with the stories of culture that air on movie screens and television. Movie clips, movie trailers, and television shows often offer story lines that can bring insight into Scripture passages or the general human experience. These visual tales can open lines of conversation in dynamic ways. People are often more comfortable discussing movies and television than Scripture. Then, when they begin to make connections between what they view on the screen and the word of God, they realize that God is revealed in the ordinary. Helping people see the connections of God and the images around them may open them to looking for evidence of theology or scriptural references in other movies and television shows. The church should not try to limit the ways God speaks to the world. Rather, the church's role is to help people discover the presence of God all around them. Connecting Scripture study with the stories of our culture helps people connect to God in real and sometimes powerful ways.

Some Bible study curriculum makes use of this type of educational experience. When working from these materials, the church is assured that the use of the suggested media is covered under a licensing package. However, if a group wishes to use a piece not included in the curriculum, it is best to study current copyright laws to ensure appropriate use.

Another option is to use the fine arts to connect the Bible to human creativity. With a computer and Internet access, we can locate paintings or mosaics from anywhere in the world and use them to give people a deeper understanding of the Bible and theology. The ancients understood the power of a picture, and so do we. The old saying, "a picture is worth a thousand words," conveys the message that pictures touch the human imagination in ways that words cannot.

Music may soothe the savage beast, and it can also speak to the human soul. Music, accessible via the Internet, adds a helpful dimension to worship, to education, and to small group studies. Music can bring people together, enlighten and inform, deepen meditation and prayer, and make us laugh.

The digital camera is another technological advance that offers ministry opportunities. A group on a mission trip can send instant pictures over the Internet, share them on a website, or show them to a group using a slide show. People at home can witness how others in the church are serving around the world. Groups can photograph their progress as well as fun events to share with the congregation.

Digital cameras are also useful in Bible studies and for developing media for use in worship or small groups. Youth especially would enjoy discussing the meaning, characters, and other aspects of a Scripture passage, then working together to create a video or slide presentation that retells the story. Digital video and cameras make the work fun but also inexpensive. Many young people already know about editing from their work in school or on community websites. Put their talent to work and display it during the Scripture reading in worship, at church meetings, and online to share with the world. It is great for children, youth, and adults to see that creative work is a valuable tool, and what they create can touch people's lives around the world.

AN AUTHENTIC MESSAGE

Whatever the church says and however it says it, the message must be authentic. We all fail Christ at one time or another. We all say or do hypocritical things sometimes. Even Paul had that problem:

> I do not understand my own actions. For I do not do what I want, but I do the very thing I hate. Now if I do what I do not want, I agree that the law is good. But in fact it is no longer I that do it, but sin that dwells within me. For I know that nothing good dwells within me, that is, in my flesh. I can will what is right, but I cannot do it. For I do not do the good I want, but the evil I do not want is what I do. Now if I do what I do not want, it is no longer I that do it, but sin that dwells within me. So I find it to be a law that when I want to do what is good, evil lies close at hand. For I delight in the law of God in my inmost self, but I see in my members another law at war with the law of my mind, making me captive to the law of sin that dwells in my members. Wretched man that I am! Who will rescue me from this body of death? Thanks be to God through Jesus Christ our Lord! So then, with my mind I am a slave to the law of God, but with my flesh I am a slave to the law of sin. (Rom 7:14-25)

Even with his failures, Paul was authentic in admitting them and authentic in his message of the nearness of the Reign of God. Paul recognized the human problem and claimed it rather than trying to hide it behind a cloak of moral certitude.

It is easy to say one thing and practice another. For the church, it is important to accept human imperfection while continuing to proclaim the good news. The church is not about being perfect, but about being relevant to the world. The church does not speak with a moral voice, but with a religious voice. The church brings God into human dialogue to invite discussion from different perspectives.

The church should be relevant to the current events of our day. With an authentic witness that is aware of culture and society, people are invited to see the presence of God. The relevant church is called to be sensitive to what happens in society, not to condemn people and be condescending toward them. The relevant church opens dialogue with people. The relevant church claims its faults while proclaiming God's acceptance and forgiveness. That is the authentic communication of the gospel in any age.

The use of technology must also be authentic. Sometimes technology may not add anything to an event. Using technology simply because it is available is not authentic. Technology is a tool that adds to the proclamation and disciple-making efforts of the church. Technology is neither the sole means nor even always the best means of making disciples. For the church's proclamation to be authentic, it has to touch people where they are. Some will find the church online, others through music, others through images, others through spiritual disciplines, and still others through missions. The church has an authentic witness on many fronts, and it has many tools with which to proclaim God's presence to the world. To reach out to all people, the church is to use all available tools. Not every congregation has every tool. Each church needs to assess its particular tools and decide what tools will work for its people. Whatever tool is used, the church is most powerful not when it is using the sledgehammer of condemnation, but rather when it is an authentic witness to the human imperfection of all people and the power of God working within that imperfection to create something new.

THE FUTURE OF TECHNOLOGY

What the future holds is, of course, completely unknown. The technological world changes so rapidly that even speculating on what comes next is fruitless. Whatever it will be, the church is called to view each advancement as a potential tool for ministry. As church people learn to consider technological advances as tools to use for God's message, they will view changes in the world and culture with expectation rather than fear.

In the biblical accounts and the history of the church, we find that the followers of God began where people were, and then God moved them to a new point. The church can now communicate the gospel to more people than the disciples or Paul ever thought possible. Can you image what Jesus and Paul could have done if they had had access to today's communication tools? If we are to be good stewards, we will follow the example of the Bible and use what is available to talk about the meaning and purpose of God in the life of the church.

A COMMUNITY OF FAITH

In the final analysis, communicating the gospel is more than using a certain kind of technology; it is more than glitz and glamour. Communicating the gospel must involve the people of the church corporately and personally. Technology is one of many tools at the church's disposal to share the gospel message, but technology is not the master or savior of the church. While technology is useful, the church is people, and the community of faith must be involved in the proclamation. The community of faith connects with people, reaches people, shares with people, and brings the gospel message to technology. The church community gives voice to the message of the good news, and God gives it life in people's lives.

To be open to God's actions in people's lives means the church community openly accepts the people God sends into the community. If guests come to the church, but no one speaks to them, welcomes them, or incorporates them into the faith community, they will not stay in the community. If the church does not help people grow in their discipleship of worship, spiritual development, and fellowship, it will not make disciples but will simply become another club people can join. The church community must work with God to make disciples. No matter what tools the church has at its disposal, at the forefront is the church community and how it welcomes and incorporates new people into the body of Christ. If people are not accepted or are excluded from the church community for some reason, then the church places a barrier between that person and God.

When the gospel story moves in the lives of people, they need a community of faith that will provide a nurturing environment for the message to grow. The community of faith that reaches out with the gospel message technologically has to be willing to live that message at the church building and beyond. People looking to understand more of the gospel and what it means to live a life in discipleship with Christ need a community that is welcoming and encouraging to all people. The church community must provide opportunities for people to discover and use the gifts God has given them for the continued spreading of the gospel message. Even with technology, the church community has an important role. Technology is the entrance door; the community of faith is the continual guide to a deeper walk with God.

The church can offer exposure to technology for all people that can help lower the gap between those who can afford it and those who can't. The time is right for the church to be a force for economic and social justice by providing opportunities that can help people learn new skills. This can be done as a ministry of the church that will proclaim the gospel message of hope in the midst of people's hopelessness.

The church has an opportunity to reach new generations in vital ways. As younger people continue to go online, the church can reach them with the gospel message in a place where they would not necessarily think of finding it. The impact of technology continues to spread in our lives. It is essential for the church to find ways of using technology to spread the gospel message to all people. Never before has it been so convenient to take the message around the world. Paul traveled by foot and ship, missionaries have spent their lives sharing the gospel in foreign lands, and now the church has a tool that can proclaim the gospel message instantly to the world.

Communicating the gospel requires a well-rounded approach. It involves God working in the lives of people who use the tools God has given. It involves the church inviting all of humankind into a meaningful relationship with God. It is an old story with new implications. It is a story that is transformative of the church and the world. It is an old story that connects with each of our lives and changes us in sometimes inexplicable ways. Relationships with God and humanity will always influence and change us. Sometimes it is a positive change, and other times it is not. But we are changed by the relationships we build.

The world is forever changing, and the message of God's love let loose in the world is a life-changing message. The church has a story to tell in any way the church can tell it. The church should not fear to tell the story, nor should it fear the variety of ways available as a means to tell the story. This is a media-driven age, and the church is called to embrace it and use it to tell the story of God's reaching out in the incarnation of Christ to a hurting and alienated world. The Internet, iPods, digital media, and other new developments in technology continue to change how humanity communicates. God has given the church a variety of tools that can reach around the world. All the church has to do is grasp the tools, put them to use, and let God reveal God's grace to the world.

NOTES

1. Computer and Internet Use in the United States: 2003, Current Population Survey Report, http://www.census.gov/prod/2005pubs/p23-208.pdf (accessed 12 June 2008).

2. "Blog" is a contraction of "weblog," which is an online journal in which people write about their activities, children, politics, current events, or other subjects and post the material for public viewing.

BIBLIOGRAPHY

Art Through the Ages. 6th edition. Revised by Horst de la Croix and Richard G. Tansey. New York: Harcourt Brace Jovanovich, Inc., 1975.

The Bible. New Revised Standard Version, 1989.

Bonhoeffer, Dietrich. *The Cost of Discipleship.* Translated by R. H. Fuller. New York: Macmillan Publishing Company, 1963.

Brueggemann, Walter. *Biblical Perspectives on Evangelism: Living in a Three Storied Universe.* Nashville: Abingdon Press, 1993.

Dowley, Tim, John Briggs, David Wright, and Robert Linder, editors. *Eerdman's Handbook to the History of Christianity,* Grand Rapids: WM. B. Eerdmans CO, 1977.

"The Electronic Ben Franklin: The Quotable Franklin." http://www.ushistory.org/franklin/quotable/singlehtml. htm (accessed 20 August 2008).

Jones, Scott. *The Evangelistic Love of God and Neighbor.* Nashville: Abingdon Press, 2003.

The United Methodist Book of Worship. The United Methodist Publishing House: Nashville, 1992.

The United Methodist Hymnal. Words by Katherine Hankey and music by William G. Fischer. The United Methodist Publishing House, 1989.

The Works of John Wesley. Volume 2. CD-ROM version. Providence House Publishers: Franklin, Tennessee, 1995.